Your Home, Your Money

How to Leverage Home Ownership
and Avoid Costly Mistakes

Your Home, Your Money

Orli Dudaie

Contents

Introduction

For most of us, housing accounts for a significant portion of our monthly budget, regardless of whether we are paying rent or a mortgage. Is this expense working to our benefit? Often, lenders advise us how much money we can borrow, a realtor finds us a dream home within this budget, and we have access to an abundance of information on the logistics of purchasing or refinancing a home. Is this the right way to carry out your home financial goals?

The way you phrase a question will often determine its answer. Is it possible to get the correct answer for the wrong question? When looking to purchase a home, you are often guided to take the first step and check how much you can qualify for. Instead of letting others tell you how much you should spend, decide what benefits you. Guide others to work together with you towards achieving what you want. As a current or aspiring homeowner, do not miss opportunities, often passed unseen.

You do not need to be a full-time real estate investor or a property manager to understand how to make your home investment work for you. Use the information in this book to maximize your home ownership potential and achieve your actual financial power. This book will give you an overview of a primary residence's financial potential, a home loan's actual cost, and the process and eligibility criteria for purchasing or refinancing a home's mortgage.

My background is varied. I was educated as an architect, and after about a decade working in the field, I shifted my focus towards real estate, working as a realtor, investor, contractor, and mortgage loan officer. I learned tremendously from my clients and work experiences. From these various viewpoints and situations, I learned how to strategically evaluate a property's potential and develop creative solutions when needed. If you cannot achieve your desired outcome, the critical questions are: Why, what should be changed, and how? Have a plan for overcoming the challenges.

After working through countless transactions, I knew I had to write this book. I wanted to share this information, but more importantly, I felt a vital piece of the real estate puzzle was missing from the information given to potential buyers or homeowners looking to refinance their mortgages. My focus is on homeowners who want to buy a home or current homeowners who do not consider themselves real estate investors; both can benefit from making advantageous financial decisions. When you decide to be a real estate investor, you learn the market, the different aspects of finance, the challenges, and the opportunities. You have a game plan. As a homeowner, you are not always aware of the financial potential, except when your property is assessed, and the home's market value increases. Want it or not, when you are a homeowner, you are already investing in a home. Your home. Would you like to know your options before making your next decision?

In his poem *The Road Not Taken*, Robert Frost wrote, "Two roads diverged in a wood, and I took the one less traveled by, and that has made all the difference."

Walking down the well-worn road, from lender's consultations to realtor's guidance, before defining your financial and personal goals is putting the cart before the horse.

Your team, a lender, and a realtor will help you immensely on this path, but even though you walk this journey together, are you certain you have chosen the right road? You can reach a destination, but is it the one that is the most convenient for you?

To be able to plan, we first must know what is possible. To have a realistic plan, we need to know the ins and outs of our real estate potential. This is what I will share with you. The options, the paths, the how, and the whys. The goals will be personal, resulting in different outcomes from one person to another.

I am inspired by the moments of revelation when a friend or a client realizes his options are different and better than initially imagined. Recently, a friend told me he is looking to buy a home in the next few months and was looking for my help listing his current home. After understanding his current situation, I asked him why he was selling. He looked at me, surprised about the question, and replied he wanted to buy another home, so he had to sell his current one. "What is there to question here?" he responded.

I asked him if he would be interested in keeping the house and buying his next one. Of course, he answered dismissively. Who wouldn't want that? But how can I afford that? We reviewed the numbers, realizing he could do that under certain circumstances. His question changed. He needed to first decide *if* he wanted to sell his home, not when to put it on the market. He would not have known it was an option if we had not reviewed the numbers and planned accordingly. After deciding what he wanted, it would be clear what path he should take. You need to know your options to make the most of your decisions and to make your dreams a reality.

One manifestation of the American dream is the accomplishment of owning a home. At what point does this dream become a reality? When you buy the home and owe most of its value to a lender, when the house is paid off, or when you make a financial profit while living there? Is the American dream a journey or a destination?

My American dream has constantly evolved. When I was renting, I wanted to purchase a home, so I did not need to move unless I wanted to. When purchasing, the home location, size, and condition did not always align with my financial goals.

Weighting all the aspects, how can we prioritize? How can we enjoy the journey without losing focus on the destination, and how can we avoid costly mistakes along the way? Do we serve the house, or does the house serves us? When we purchase a home, it often serves our needs considering the location, the size, the physical characteristics of the home, and, of course, the price; otherwise, we would not buy it. As life evolves, our needs change, and it is beneficial to re-evaluate if, at any given time, you are positioning yourself in the place that most benefits you.

The purchase of your home is not the mountain's peak. You should not rest on your laurels after conquering this milestone. You achieved a dream and bought your home. You will need to draw the mountain's peak, where you would like to be, on a more advanced path of this journey, not at the beginning before repair bills add up and the property taxes increase. They always do.

We will simplify critical aspects so you can decide how much money you should borrow, as it is not always the maximum amount you can afford. You will prioritize your needs and wants. With your exit strategy in hand and an understanding of the home's market value analysis, you will define the home search criteria that are most convenient for you. You will continue making your monthly housing payment. Still, you must be capable of looking at the much bigger picture of your financial goals, letting the next decision be powerful enough to lead you to your long-term targets.

Your Home, Your Money is built on five steps, covering all you need to know to maximize your home ownership financial potential. We will begin by jumping into the depth of the subject matter and review the wealth possibilities home ownership entails. This will help you frame the big picture of your possibilities, followed by information about the properties, the financing, and the home purchasing. Why should we speak about the end result first? Because your goals should strategically guide your thoughts and decisions.

> Let me share with you what happened when I thought my husband and I should refinance our current home's mortgage. I wanted to refinance, as rates had come down since we originated the mortgage. There were very promising options. I wanted to share my point of view with my husband, so we sat at the kitchen table, where I neatly organized five amortization schedules in front of us, detailing all the options. I intended to review it all, brainstorm various options, and determine our best direction. About a minute and a half, after I began comparing all the numbers in the charts, my husband stopped looking at the papers. He was just staring at me. "What?" I asked, a little bit impatient. He smiled and said, "Please, just get to the point. What is our best option?"

I know that some of us love numbers and would prefer to understand concepts and review different scenarios with numbers, while others, like my husband, do not want to see all the possible examples. My husband would prefer to know facts that benefit him, understand the complete process, and move on. To address this, I depict scenarios with number analyses to help those that prefer to skip it.

At the end of the book, you will find a Glossary with helpful terminology. The first time a word or concept explained in the glossary appears in the text, it will be marked in bold to guide you about the further information available in the glossary.

By the end of every step, you will have the opportunity to write down thoughts, takeaways, and items for your to-do list. It is for your benefit to articulate those needs, preferences, and goals. Remember, the realtor and the mortgage loan officer can help you better if you have set your personal goals first.

By the time you finish reading the book:

- ♦ You can have your goals defined along with your timeline.
- ♦ You can define the property you are looking for and the property contingency plan if you're not buying your forever home.
- ♦ You will know how to position yourself better financially before applying for a mortgage.
- ♦ You will have a clear sense of the entire purchasing process.
- ♦ You will know what to do next in this exciting journey.

For more information, go to www.AskOrli.com

Preface

We often hear that everything happens for a reason, but when unexpected things do happen, it is hard for me to find comfort in these words. When I was young and was told, "Everything will be OK," the only thought that passed my mind back then was, "How do you know?"

I want to share with you the time I realized I needed to write this book and my *why*. The time I realized that everything *did* happen to me for a reason. For that purpose, you will need to join me through virtual traveling, cultures, and adventures.

I moved through continents and countries, changed languages and professions, and while my various paths all appear very different, they all, in fact, complemented each other. Today, I appreciate how my experiences, successes, and challenges provided me with the toolbox I have today.

I was born in Argentina and raised in Israel. My husband and I studied at a university in Mexico City, even though upon arrival, neither of us had any extended family or friends living there. I understood Spanish but had not spoken it for years. My husband did not know a word of Spanish. He used to record his classes during his first two years of school to be able to review the lessons, in Spanish, of course. Some friends told us we were out of our minds, but at that time, we enjoyed our student life, creating beautiful friendships. We did not understand why our actions were perceived as illogical.

Yes, we had decided to travel, and if it did not work out, we would rethink our path. Not a big deal, or at least this is what we thought when we were in our early twenties.

I studied architecture and art history, specialized in surrealism art, and enjoyed Mexican architecture and culture. After completing our studies, we returned to Israel, where I focused on both single-family and commercial construction, design, and on-site construction supervision. Parallel to my work as an architect, I volunteered in several organizations, some of which participated in joint educational projects with organizations in the U.S. After a few years in Israel, I was invited by an American organization to relocate to the U.S. for three years, and even though the work sounded very exciting, it was a hard decision. The offer would require me to quit my job and put my professional career as an architect on hold. I was six months pregnant with my third child, my older boys were still in elementary school, and my husband would be required to quit his job in the hospital.

Somehow, we managed to block out our fears and doubts and simply follow our gut. This was very uncommon for me, as I am usually a rational, stubborn person. For as long as I can remember, I have always questioned what I do and why I do it, and I have always sought alternative ways and paths. This time, the decision involved my entire family. However, they supported the decision to move. We were excited about our upcoming journey and determined to ignore the noise of doubt. We relocated to the U.S., settled in New Jersey, and three years quickly turned into five. Everyone was busy; my baby boy was about to begin first grade in school. It was time to move on; it was time for me to return to architecture.

I am passionate about real estate, from the design stages to full construction, acquiring property, and enhancing it to achieve its full potential. In the following years, we remained in New Jersey. I worked as an architect and a realtor and began some home renovation projects. A few years down the road, I shifted my focus more to home renovations and real estate investing. Since I am a numbers person, I was intrigued to learn more about the financial aspect of real estate. I earned my mortgage loan officer license and worked with clients on refinancing their mortgages. Looking at my past experiences, it was a perfect combination. Numbers need to work for the client's convenience, and it all combined to find a way to ensure that each client is in the best position to achieve their goals.

The countless conversations I've had with clients as a mortgage loan officer made me realize that there is vital information that many people need to know. As a real estate investor, there were diverse opportunities that were clear to my peers and me, but as homeowners, there was much to be learned. As I thought about the topics and details most important to share, I could never find the time to write. The fast pace of life makes it all too difficult to stop to reevaluate priorities, as the list of excuses remains ever long. Had I been asked, I could have provided many reasons why it was not a good time for me to slow down; however, one phone call changed everything. I got a call early one morning about a family member's medical emergency, and two hours later, I was on my way to the airport, thinking I would be back in a week. That week turned into multiple weeks, which turned into months. It was three months before I returned home to the U.S. Yes, life can stop, and when it does, it is not always by choice.

Medical emergencies can push your boundaries and make you realize that time is precious, reinforcing the importance of consciously navigating your life, prioritizing your goals, leaving room for your passions, and finding a way to make it all work. I had to make it work.

Financial goals seem boring on the surface, but I remember specific clients, their life stories, and how these very decisions impacted them. Some stories are impossible to forget. I knew I wanted to write this book when I came back to the U.S. I knew it in my gut, just as I knew so many years before that moving to the U.S. was the right thing for our family. No excuses. No delays.

STEP 1
ACCUMULATING WEALTH

"Knowledge is power; you hear it all the time, but knowledge is not power. It's only potential power. It only becomes power when multiplied by action." – Jim Kwik

Financial wealth is generally defined as an abundance of valuable possessions or money. You are the only one who can define what it means for you. Goals and desires vary from one person to another. For some people, it can be the security of owning a home free and clear from a mortgage, and others would prefer a rental income for their retirement. There are endless options and solutions.

Let me share two experiences I had with my youngest son, Amir, when he was nine. We went on a volunteer trip to an orphanage in Costa Rica, living with a local host family in Santa Barbara. The family included Adela, a single mother in her forties, her mother, and her three kids. Every morning, Amir and I would take the bus, which was about a twenty-minute ride. After another relatively short walk on a dirt track, we would arrive at Al Niño Con Cariño, a local orphanage serving as a home for girls aged six to sixteen. I taught English while Amir worked with the younger girls in arts and crafts projects he brought from the U.S. During recess, Amir ran around, playing with the girls on the playground. One day, he shared with me that he did not understand why the girls often told him that he was "bendito;" he was blessed. I asked him: "Do you know your parents?" "Do you have a home where you live?" "Do you feel safe?"

He bowed his little head and quietly answered, "I understand."

On the way back to the bus station, we walked through a tin shack, and in the open entrance stood a very young boy, about three years old. He had shorts, no shirt, and was standing barefoot on the sand floor. He was smiling, looking quite pleased. I told Amir I was thinking of how wonderful it was, that despite his rugged surroundings the young kid was so happy. Amir looked at me from under his green umbrella; he did not smile and told me that I was wrong. He continued his explanation, "This boy does not know that there is something better, so why should he try and fight to get to a better place in life?"

I was left speechless. I thought I was teaching a nine-year-old some life lessons, but we shared the teaching.

You decide your own comfort level and goals. In the same way that the answer varies from person to person, you probably will not provide the same responses in your twenties, thirties, or fifties. As life evolves, you will reevaluate your direction as needed.

We are focusing here on home ownership. Most of us have a limited income and need to make prudent budget choices. You spend the money regardless, whether paying rent or a mortgage, so it should be the option that best allows you to achieve your goals. You often hear that your home is your biggest asset. This is accurate if your home generates income, but usually, this is not the case. You can gain more value by either spending more or spending less. You can evaluate your assets based on their actual cost, understand their future value, and manage your debts to minimize unnecessary expenses. You, too, can benefit from real estate tax deductions and plan for a future asset capital gain or rental income. You can benefit from each one of these paths, or you can benefit from them all.

The following four chapters explain the opportunities for wealth building through home ownership. We'll begin by explaining two concepts essential to understanding property wealth: home **equity** and **appreciation**.

Equity is the difference between the home's fair market value and the outstanding balance of all liens on the property. If your home value is $300,000 and you owe $220,000, your home equity is $80,000. Home appreciation is when a property increases its value over a period of time.

These concepts will be used when analyzing your actions and future results, as you have financial options to minimize the initial equity you contribute at the time of a property purchase. The **primary residence** will accumulate wealth as you pay down the debt while possibly increasing its value over time due to appreciation. Not every contribution will impact your equity the same way. Managing debt can save you substantial money, which can be reflected by paying less interest on the property's loan or using the home equity to consolidate your debt. Rental income options and the tax benefits associated with it apply whether you buy a **single-family** or a **multi-family** primary residence. You will learn the criteria for home appreciation, regardless of market conditions, to ultimately increase your home's equity.

STEP 1 includes:

Chapter 1:
Primary
Residence

Chapter 2:
Home
Equity

Chapter 3:
Debt
Cost

Chapter 4:
Rental
Income

Primary Residence

Buying a home for the first time is exciting. From the search phase to the actual purchase, even though it can feel tedious until you move into the house. As someone who has moved houses multiple times, let me share that this unique feeling does not fade as you move into your second, third, or even fourth home. After all, each home encompasses your dreams and aspirations at that point in time. There is a unique moment after you sign the documents at the **closing table**, receive the keys to your new home, and make those first steps as you pass through the door of your new house. Everything is usually quiet and empty. Just you and the property, waiting to become your home. Take a deep breath and enjoy this moment.

As the homeowner of your primary residence, you are entitled to several benefits, most of which do not apply to an investment property. Here are the three things you need to know, and any detailed information regarding loans will be reviewed in the later financial chapters.

1. Primary residence definition

When you ask for a primary residence loan, you are expected to live in the house for at least twelve months. Whether it's a single-family house, **condo**, or multi-family, if you live there and can prove it, it's your primary residence. After a year or more, you can move out, sell or rent this home, and purchase your next primary residence as long as you intend to move into this new home.

Your primary residence can be any property of up to four units. Yes, you can buy the building of three or four units as a primary residence and live in one unit while renting the other units. This distinction is essential, as primary residence loans have better terms than investment property loans. If, when you move out, you decide to keep the property and rent it, you can continue to benefit from keeping your primary residence loan. If you **refinance** your mortgage after you move out, it will be considered an investment property.

If you buy your second/vacation home, you can qualify for a **conventional loan**, often with the same advantages as a primary residence **mortgage**. The lender defines a second home as a property you purchase in addition to your current home. Lenders will set specific requirements to differentiate between a second home and an investment property. As definitions and loan terms vary from one lender to the other, shop around and compare.

Government mortgages can be very beneficial for primary residences; they are less restrictive in credit and debt limits. Those loans are strictly for primary residences and will not be considered for second or vacation homes.

2. Get loans with a lower down payment

The **down payment** is the cash the buyer pays upfront in a real estate transaction. It is defined as a percentage of the purchase price. You can get primary residence loans with much lower down payment compared to investment loans, in some cases as low as 3%, 3.5%, or 5%, depending on each loan criteria. There are also some loans with no money down. In an investment property loan, you often are required to have a minimum of a 25% down payment. It is a significant difference; for many, it will determine whether they can buy the property.

SCENARIO ANALYSIS: THE DOWN PAYMENT

If you want to buy a duplex at $350,000, you will be required to have a 25% minimum down payment as an investor. For the above purchase price, you will need $87,500. If you intend to move into one of the units and rent the other one, the duplex is considered a primary residence, and you might qualify for a loan with a 3% down payment of $10,500, a 5% down payment of $17,500, or even $0 down payment. After a year or two, you can move on to another home, rent your unit, and keep paying the mortgage, keeping the additional income from renting the unit where you used to live. This approach is known as home hacking.

3. Tax benefits

Some of your primary home expenses are **tax-deductible**. Property taxes, mortgage **interest** payments, **discount points** to lower your interest rate on a new loan, some home improvement projects, home office expenses, and more can be used. Do not underestimate the power of tax deductions.

When you sell your primary home and gain money from its appreciation, under certain limitations, you can enjoy a **tax exemption** on the **capital gain**.

For example, if you bought your home five years ago at $300,000 and you put a down payment of 20% ($60,000 down payment and $240,000 loan). In those five years, you paid your mortgage down to $210,000. Let's assume you sold your home for $350,000; even though you will receive $140,000 after paying off the mortgage (less the **closing costs**), you have $50,000 of capital gain, and theoretically, you would have been required to pay taxes on this profit.

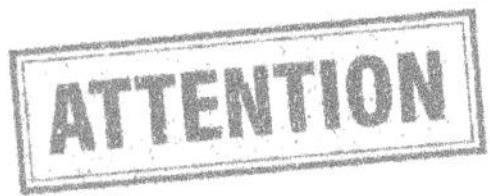

When you sell the primary home where you have lived for at least two of the last five years, if you have a capital gain from the said sale, you may qualify to exclude up to $250,000 of that gain from your income if you are single, or up to $500,000 of that gain if you file a joint return with your spouse.

If you buy a multi-family residence, the lender will consider the property a primary residence if you occupy one of the units. For tax purposes, the other units you rent out are considered investment properties, allowing you even greater savings, as these units' proportional value, excluding the land's value, can be depreciated over 27.5 years. **Depreciation** is a reduction in the value of an asset over time due to normal wear and tear. The property's actual market value can increase, and you calculate the property's depreciation as a loss for *tax purposes*.

How can it make sense that a lender approaches your multi-family home as a non-investment property, and for tax purposes, you address some units at the same property as an investment? It is simple. The two entities have different approaches and different goals. Your tax obligations are not relevant to the lender as long as they do not impact your ability to repay your debt. For tax calculations, the **terms of your loan** and the amount of your down payment are irrelevant. The only information affecting your tax obligations is the income or loss for tax purposes, and real estate has significant tax incentives.

SCENARIO ANALYSIS: DEPRECIATION

You bought a property for $250,000. When renting it, you want to calculate the depreciation for tax purposes. You begin by dividing how much of this amount is the value of the land and how much is the actual property's value. Often, you use the 20-80 ratio. We calculate 80% of the purchase to find the structure value. In this case, it is $200,000 (80% of $250,000).

As the property can be depreciated over 27.5 years, we divide $200,000 by 27.5 years = $7,272 a year. This amount can be depreciated yearly against your income for the next 27.5 years.

You need to pay income tax on your rental income. However, due to the tax benefits of your rental property, you can deduct from your income the actual expenses, the tax deductions of mortgage interest and property taxes, and finally, the property's depreciation. Your balance, for tax purposes, can show a loss when your actual balance is a surplus.

Another possible tax-saving strategy utilizes property taxes if your state has **homestead** tax exemptions. For tax purposes, a homestead is defined as a property used as the owner's principal residence. In some states, you can qualify as a homeowner for lower property tax payments. Although, just as you gain from this discount while living in the house, the property tax will increase when you move out and rent the property, as you won't be eligible to benefit from the owner-occupied discount.

I worked with a client who was offered an excellent deal for refinancing the mortgage on an investment property he had bought one year prior. As part of the process, the underwriting team checked with the township to determine the amount of property taxes due for the upcoming year, as the client asked to escrow the property taxes and home insurance. The amount of money needed to be put aside for the escrow did not make sense for my client. He knew the previous owner had paid about $1,500/year in property taxes, yet he was asked to escrow the equivalent amount for $10,000/year just for the property taxes alone. Unfortunately, the underwriting team was not wrong. The combination of canceling the owner-occupied tax discount with the appreciation of the property after the client's recent rehab had brought the actual property taxes to $10,000/year.

Take advantage of buying a home to live with a lower or no down payment, let renters pay your loan after you have already moved out, or from the start if it is a multi-family home. Utilize tax deductions and benefit from tax exclusions.

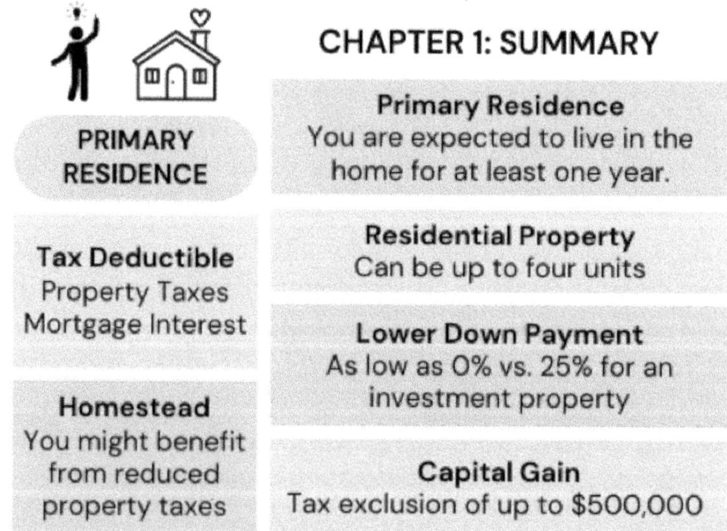

CHAPTER 2

Home Equity

I want to share why I wish I had known about home equity and its potential when we decided to sell our first home.

I was thirty-two years old with two young boys. My husband and I saved for the down payment and scheduled a meeting with a loan officer to learn about our mortgage options. We thought we had taken the right steps, as the banker advised us about the amount we could qualify to borrow and how much we needed for a down payment. We soon found an apartment that could fit our needs in a nice neighborhood with all-new construction. I remember wishing we could afford the first-floor apartment instead of the second-floor we chose, as it had a backyard that would have been wonderful for the boys. As it was more expensive, we didn't consider it an option and simply moved on. We lived in the second-floor apartment for five years and then traveled abroad for work. We knew we would be away for a few years, so we rented the apartment. The apartment has appreciated significantly since we purchased it. We ended up selling the apartment when we needed some money, following advice not to continue dealing with tenants as it was a burden; and besides, we needed the money, right? Since then, the apartment has tripled its value, but we no longer own it.

If we had understood the market and the finances and put our goals ahead to lead our decisions, we would have known that we had many more options. We didn't know our choices, and we didn't know what questions to ask. We were not aware that we did not know our options.

Home appreciation is the increase over time in property value. It results from inflation, the job market in your area, and other factors impacting the home price market. Appreciation or depreciation (decrease in home value) is specific to the market conditions of the subject property and can vary from one area to the other.

Everyone hopes their home will appreciate over time, but this is not the measurable tool you need to ensure you accumulate wealth. Your home can have a high **market value** and low cash equity. The difference between what your home is worth to your debts related to the house will determine how much money you have in equity of the home. This is the real wealth you have in the home.

For example, if you bought a home a year ago at $550,000, your mortgage is $520,000, and you spent another $35,000 on a fence and a nice patio in the backyard. You can enjoy a beautiful home, but for that given time, you might have spent more on the home than its value unless the home appreciated in the last year since you purchased it. We desire the property to increase its value while paying down the debt, so the equity in the home increases over time, increasing your wealth.

It is important to learn the factors impacting the current home value to make more knowledgeable decisions on home appreciation estimation, regardless of aspects we cannot control, such as general market trends. You can use this information to not overpay on the purchase unless it is for your benefit or as you desire. You should estimate in advance an **after-repair value** (ARV) if you renovate your home, so you do not overpay, or from the planning stages, because your target is to earn a profit when you sell. All these, combined with the debt payment understanding, will help you target the home equity's increase.

I would like to emphasize that you are not expected to do the realtor's or the appraiser's work. By sharing this information, I hope you understand the concepts and the approach to a home's value to better understand the potential when you are touring a home or considering home renovations.

We will review two concepts to calculate a home's value:

- ◆ Comparable properties
- ◆ Price per square foot

COMPARABLE PROPERTIES

To determine the current home market value, an appraiser compares what properties were sold in the area in the last six months, up to twelve months if needed, and up to a mile radius from the subject property. Suppose the appraiser does not have the right comparable in that radius, the search area is further examined, assuring that the results do not impact the accuracy of the market value. The properties must be compatible with the kind of property (single-family, condominium, townhome, etc.), the style (ranch, multilevel, two stories, colonial, etc.), the school zone, and other criteria. Each of the properties has a different finish level; some are up to date, some are renovated, and others are dated and need some love and renovations. In addition, each property can have elements that benefit the user or decrease the value, such as a finished basement, back yard, busy streets vs. a cul-de-sac, or other desired fixtures. When the appraiser gathers the properties that are the best-sold comparables, he/she compares their price per square foot and adjusts the comparable sold properties to the subject property. Usually, three to five comps are used. For this reason, comparing only the market price can be deceiving if the size, style, and condition of the properties compared are not the same.

PRICE PER SQUARE FOOT

If you are searching for a house, looking at an asking price is not enough. A house might appear to be at a reasonable market price when you compare it to other houses sold in the neighborhood, but when you compare the price per square foot (sq. ft.), you get a totally different perspective.

A price per sq. ft. is determined by the home price divided by the sq. ft. of the finished area above ground. You should not include the garage, basement, balconies, or screened porches in the sq. ft. calculations. There are other considerations with a split level and an atrium ranch (when you have one level open to the lower level); however, as a rule of thumb, you should calculate the entry-level area and up, not the living area sq. ft., which could include any finished area.

WHY DO YOU NEED TO KNOW THIS?

- Understand actual market value
- Understand the potential and its impact on home equity

A home at $360,000 with 1800 sq. ft. is more expensive than a $396,000 home with 2,200 sq. ft. The first one is $200/ sq. ft., and the other is $180 / sq. ft. It might be worth it. It depends if there are other features, lot characteristics, or finish levels that justify it. This is key to understanding appreciation potential and your level of comfort.

Many times, when speaking with clients about their current home value, in addition to being aware of what was sold in their area, the clients were calculating how much they invested in the home, expecting that the value of the home would increase by at least as much money as they had invested, sometimes including yard work, paint, windows repairs, new carpet, etc. Unfortunately, it does not work that way. When you compare the price per sq. ft. in your area to a similar property, you will see an evident price range per sq. ft. according to the finish level: i.e., new, totally renovated, up-to-date, and move-in ready, although the kitchen and/or bathrooms might benefit from a renovation.

Usually, painting or changing the carpet will not elevate the property's price to the next finish level. On the other hand, by closing a screen porch and integrating it with the home, you add sq. ft. to the property, and the value will increase. You also might target specific renovations when walking the property. Before purchasing the home, you need to be aware of this and decide if this is a path you want to pursue.

CHAPTER 2: SUMMARY

Paying Down The Home's Debt

Home Market Value
Comparable of sold properties,
last six months

Home Appreciation
Increase in the home's value over a period of time

CHAPTER 3
Debt Cost Management

I remember buying a car with my oldest son. A few days prior, on the morning of his twenty-first birthday, my sons were on their way to college in two separate cars as they continued to different places afterward. While exiting the highway, one brother rear-ended the other. It resulted in the total loss of one car and severe damage to the other car. No, it is not a joke. Physically, my boys were okay, but the two vehicles were not so lucky.

Discussing with my son in advance his purchase options, we told him the amount of money we were planning on spending was about $14,000. He would take a loan, check the options presented to him, how many years of repayment were involved, and compare the interest rates. As we parked, a salesman immediately approached us. He was eager to find my son the perfect car. I was a parent supporting two kids in college and emphasized that we did not want to exceed $14,000 as the purchase price, with a maximum five-year loan. I was impressed by this young man's ability to shift the focus from my son's concerns to the excitement of a new car. Explaining that money was not an issue, as the purchase price did not matter, all my son needed to tell him was how much he wanted to spend per month. The salesman added that he was confident he could get a special deal from his manager and that everything would work out.

I interrupted the conversation, clarifying that I did not want to exceed the $14,000 purchase price and that the purchase price did indeed matter. The young man stood firm, looked at me, turned to my son, and told him that I did not understand. He could get a seven- or ten-year loan; all my son needed to tell him was what monthly payment he wanted to pay, and the number of payments would be arranged accordingly. He looked firmly at my son, pointed at one of the cars my son liked, and asked him, "You want it, right?"

I was bothered observing how this industry professional tried to deceive my son. Using the estimated monthly payments of a $14,000 loan over five years, he could sell him a much more expensive car and make him commit to a longer-than-desired term. The actual cost, with interest, would have exceeded our original plan. That would have been fine if only my son had been aware of this. It is important to make knowledgeable decisions and understand the full magnitude of our actions. More challenging than this is to know whom to listen to and who to ignore. Who is on our side versus who looks like he is on our side, helping us to get what we want using his/her professional experience when in reality, all the professional experience is targeted to achieve one goal: to help the professional make more money in sales of product or services.

We left the car dealership and bought a VW Jetta at another dealership, where my son not only found a car he liked, but also we were not pushed to make a decision that did not align with our plan.

I often feel that when we think about home payments, the experience bears similarities to what happened at the car dealership. Buyers are asked what property they want, and home buyers, or homeowners refinancing their mortgage, tend to focus on the monthly payment, regardless of whether or not it is truly to their advantage.

Paying debt is not a way to accumulate wealth unless someone else pays your debt. A renter paying your mortgage so you can increase your home equity or end up with a free and clear home, for example. We will focus on understanding the cost of the debt related to your home so you can save when possible. In overall personal finance, you get to keep more money by saving money on unnecessary payments.

You need to know your comfort level and convenience of your monthly home expenses and how this impacts the true cost of your loan. Let's review:

True mortgage debt cost
The term of a loan
The impact of $100
Putting your debt-ducks in a row

1. True mortgage debt cost

When we buy something, we look at the price tag to decide if it is worth it and if we can afford it. With a property, we use the sale price to evaluate if this property is worth the price requested, and we review the monthly payment to ensure we can afford this payment. There is a difference between the sale price in the contract when you buy the home and how much the property will actually cost you. To understand what you pay in your monthly mortgage payments and how it impacts your home's price tag, we will begin with some key concepts:

Principal is the amount you borrow and have to pay back. Especially in the first years of a loan, you can feel comfortable sending significant payments to the lender, and you assume your debt is being paid down accordingly. How much of the money you pay monthly goes towards paying down your debt? If you borrowed $200,000 and sent your lender $1,400 a month, the debt will not be reduced by $1,400 or even $1,000 a month. In a thirty-year loan at a 5% interest rate, the first month, only $240 will be paid towards the principal, paying down your debt!

Interest is your payment to your lender to cover the cost of the loan. The interest is calculated as a percentage of the principal balance. In the example used above, from the $1,400 paid monthly, the first month, $833 will be paid towards interest. This does not benefit you; it is the cost of the loan.

Escrow is the monthly payment you send to the lender to cover some of the costs associated with home ownership, such as real estate taxes, home insurance premiums, and private mortgage insurance costs. In the example above, if you pay $1,400 per month, and your principal and interest payments total $1,073, the difference of $327 will be paid towards other expenses.

The term of a loan is the time you have to repay your loan.

Mortgage Refinance is when you replace your current mortgage with a new one with more favorable terms or other benefits you can achieve in this transaction.

The loan amount, the term of the loan, and the interest rate will determine your monthly payment of principal and interest. Some loans are interest only. It means you pay the lender the interest payments, and the debt amount remains the same. More common are mortgage payments, where your monthly payment covers the principal and the interest. Sometimes, the monthly loan payments will include principal and interest only, and you will independently cover the property taxes and homeowners' insurance payments. Some will require you to pay the lender an escrow to cover property taxes, home insurance, or other expenses such as mortgage insurance.

In continuation, when we compare the true mortgage debt cost, we will compare only the principal and interest (P&I) payments. You pay property taxes and home insurance regardless of whether you have a mortgage.

In a fixed-interest rate mortgage, even though you will be charged the same monthly amount, the monthly repayment amount is split between the principal and interest, changing monthly. Each month the payment of the principal will increase, and the interest will decrease, resulting in the same total amount. Understanding the allocation of your monthly mortgage payments will help you strategize your actions, as your equity will grow slower in the initial years of a loan.

$200,000 loan, 30-year term, 5% interest

Month:	Principal	Interest	Total
1	$240	$834	$1,074
60	$307	$767	$1,074
120	$394	$680	$1,074
180	$506	$568	$1,074

Suppose you see a house at $250,000; you want to put down 20% of the cost and borrow the other 80%, which is $200,000. The price is fair, and you decide to proceed with the purchase. Would you feel the same if I told you that you would pay $436,000 or more for this house? Would you still be interested in proceeding and purchasing the house? You work hard for your money, and this is a big difference. (This is what you will pay for a 30-year loan at a 5% interest rate).

What if you are not planning on staying in the house for 30 years and paying off the mortgage? Let's say you expect to stay in the house for five years, and your plan is to pay the mortgage for five years, sell the house, and then use the equity of your home to buy your next home. In the mortgage scenario mentioned above, the monthly payment is $1074 (P&I).

It sounds promising if, after five years, your payment to your lender totaled $64,440. Conventional thinking says you would believe you are doing the right thing, as you own a home, investing in your biggest asset, and if possible, you will reduce the interest rate in order to save money. The lower the interest rate, the better, right? 

How much of this amount, was interest payments, and how much was allocated to reduce your loan? In this scenario, the $64,400 paid over five years was divided: $16,343 to the principal and $48,057 to the interest.

Let's continue with the scenario above. During those five years, you refinanced once. It looked very beneficial to you; you got a lower interest rate, you did not have to worry about the closing costs, as they were not out of pocket because they were rolled into the loan, and you skipped one monthly mortgage payment after refinancing. This means you get a lower interest rate, and your debt increases. At the end of the five years, you sell your home and have expenses (realtor's fee, closing costs, and others). On the other hand, maybe the home appreciated significantly. Was the refinance beneficial? Find out the details in the scenario analysis.

Remember, the loan amounts, length of the loan, interest rates, and loan costs are hypothetical, with the only purpose of understanding the process, the financial impact, and the logic of this. You will do your own calculation to reflect your mortgage, your numbers, and your terms.

SCENARIO ANALYSIS: WHAT IS THE PROFIT?

- Property: $250,000

- Down Payment: 20% = $50,000

- Mortgage: 30 years, at 5% interest rate, $1,074 P&I

- Refinance after three years, another 30 years, at 4% interest rate. $4,500 closing costs were rolled into the loan.

- After five years of ownership, the home appreciated 10%, and you sold the house at $275,000. You had $2,000 in closing costs.

- You paid the realtor 5% and spent $3,000 in repairs before putting your home on the market.

What is your profit?

- You originally invested the 20% down payment: $50,000.

- Assuming you did not pay additional payments during the first three years, the debt amount is as follows:

    Principal after three years: $190,687

    Adding $4,500 refinance cost

    The new loan amount when refinancing: $195,187

- The monthly payment was reduced to $932, saving $142 monthly.

- The balance of the new loan after two years from refinancing: $191,749.

Let's calculate:

$275,000 sale price—$13,750 Realtor fee—$3,000 repairs—$191,749 debt balance—$2,000 closing costs = $66,501. You gained just above $16,000 over the amount you invested if the home appreciated by $25,000.

You can interpret these numbers in a few ways:

- You earned $16,000, and this gain is tax-exempt. This can be a higher or lower number based on actual market appreciation.

- If the house did not appreciate the 10%, you could break even or be at a loss, even though you spent $61,104 ($1,074x36 months and $932x24 months).

- The refinance theoretically sounded very convenient, but comparing how much your monthly expense was reduced to the cost of the loan, you did not break even to offset the savings with the cost of the loan.

   Your saved $142 monthly: 24 months x $142 savings = $3,408

   Your refinance cost you $4,500.

You must realize that what looks convenient at first will not necessarily benefit you. Each case needs to be analyzed with your options, rates, costs, needs, and goals.

 **Takeaways:**

- You need to know your loan numbers and financial goals before taking action on a mortgage. It is a must. You will need to answer yourself: Does what I do now, financially, lead me toward achieving my financial goals?

- Theoretical and wishful thinking is just that. A theory. You can benefit significantly from a market appreciation, but when you do your math, stick to the facts you know now. To plan on appreciation because you are renovating and increasing the property's value in the current market is very different from assumptions. Do not accept or justify a future theory just because the current numbers and your future capital gain sound theoretically beneficial.

- Let the numbers talk. When calculating the amount you spend on mortgage interest, remember to calculate how much you save with the tax benefits. The bottom line will reflect the actual cost of the property.

2. The term of a loan

A term of a loan is the number of years you have to pay back the loan. Common loan terms are 30, 20, and 15 years, and some lenders offer any number of years between eight and thirty. What are the impacts of choosing a loan's term besides knowing when a loan will be paid off?

The more years you have on your mortgage, the lower your monthly payment will be because you stretch out the time to pay off the mortgage. Along with this benefit, you will have a higher interest cost, as you are paying the interest for longer.

I remember speaking about mortgage terms with a lovely woman in her eighties who wanted to refinance. She was laughing, saying she could not care less about the term and was not looking to pay the mortgage off; the only impactful fact for her was the monthly payment. There are no right or wrong decisions; however, it is essential to be fully informed to choose the best option for you.

The shorter the term, the better interest rate you get. This is an excellent incentive to have a shorter term, with the downside of the higher monthly payments. The market rates will determine the actual interest rate for the specific loan you get. For example, for a $200,000 loan, you will pay monthly (P&I):

30-year, 5% interest rate:	$1,074
30-year, 4.5% interest rate:	$1,013
30-year, 4% interest rate:	$955
20-year, 4% interest rate:	$1,212
20-year 3.5% interest rate:	$1,160
20-year 3% interest rate:	$1,109
15-year 4% interest rate:	$1,479
15-year 3% interest rate:	$1,381
15-year 2.5% interest rate:	$1,334

Those interest rates are hypothetical, as the market shifts constantly. You should pay attention to the fact that the cost per month of a 15-year loan is higher than a 30-year loan, even if compared at the same interest rate (compare the 4%), but it is not doubled, even though you will pay off the mortgage in half the time. As the interest rate is lower with the shorter term, the mortgage payment will be reduced even further.

We mentioned previously that a home can be an asset or a liability, depending on who pays the debt; you or someone else. If you rent your home instead of selling it, you might prefer the 30-year mortgage, and the total interest paid to the lender will be higher. On the other hand, the lower monthly payment will allow the rent income to cover the property expenses.

There is a difference between the term determined in the loan structure, on paper, and the actual options to pay off a loan.

When you are set with a monthly payment, you can never pay less, as you will be in default. You can pay more every month, which means you send your lender more money than what you are required to send. The additional payment will be applied directly to the principal, thus:

- reducing the debt balance,
- reducing the remaining length of the loan,
- reducing the total interest paid to the lender.

If you want to pay more, why not choose a different term? Instead of 30 years, do a 20-year loan or another term, and benefit from a lower interest rate.

If you feel comfortable with the monthly commitment, go for it. If you decide on a particular term and plan on sending more money monthly, there are two main aspects to consider: flexibility and discipline.

Flexibility:

You can have a 30-year mortgage loan and send additional monthly payments. The loan will be paid off sooner, and you can set up a direct electronic payment, so you do not forget. You know that if there are unforeseen circumstances and for a few months you prefer to lower your mortgage payment back to the original amount of the

30-year loan, without the additional payment, you can. This gives you peace of mind, as you do not want to default on mortgage payments.

Discipline:

What is the downside of the above? Discipline. Are you goal-oriented and disciplined enough to follow through even though no one obligates you?

When doing refinances, I often heard from clients the desire "not to go back with the mortgage." For example, if they got a 30-year mortgage eight years ago and have 22 years remaining on the mortgage, they do not want to refinance to any mortgage term that will add years to their remaining 22-year term. I understand this point of view. The good news is that you can decide what term you want, and you are not obligated to refinance to the previous original term. Of course, this needs to be reviewed to ensure you are eligible.

SCENARIO ANALYSIS:
REFINANCE TO SHORTEN THE LOAN'S TERM

Eight years ago, you took a $300,000 loan for 30 years at a 5% interest rate. The monthly P&I payment is $1,610. If you did not make any extra payments, the balance should be $257,559.

If you refinance, adding $4,441 for closing costs, the total new loan amount will be $262,000. Let's check two refinance options:

- 20 years, at 4% interest, will result in a $1,588 monthly payment.

- 15 years at 3.5% interest will result in a $1,874 monthly payment.

Let's calculate:

In the 20-year option, you reduced your monthly payment by $22 and reduced your mortgage by two years! It is definitely a win-win. In the 15-year option, you increased your monthly payment by $264 and reduced your mortgage by seven years.

Another comparison between the 20- and 15-year options is the total interest paid during the life of the loan:

- 20 years, at 4% interest, total interest paid: $119,040.

- 15 years at 3.5% interest, total interest paid: $75,139.

You will determine the best term option based on the need to reduce the monthly payment, pay the mortgage faster, or pay less overall interest to the lender.

 **Takeaways:**

♦ Will your budget dictate the plan and term that is possible for you, or is there room to re-arrange your budget? Can you compare different terms and their impact?

♦ Is flexibility essential for you? Based on your income and expenses, if property taxes and home insurance increase, and they usually do, will you find yourself in a stressful financial situation?

♦ Do you consider yourself to have enough discipline to follow a plan if you want the actual loan payments to be different from the payment you are obligated to per contract?

3. The impact of $100

Do you think $100 per month can have a substantial financial impact? Let's do some quick math using the loan details of a $200,000 loan.

- A $200,000 loan, 30 years, 5% interest = Your monthly payment is $1074.
- Your total interest for the life of the loan will be $186,512.
- Add $100 to your monthly payment. You send your lender $1,174.
- Your mortgage will be paid off after 24 years and 10 months.
- Your total interest will be reduced to $149,443, saving $37,069.

Imagine shortening the mortgage by five years and two months, not paying the $1,074 monthly payment. During the life of the loan, you paid $29,800 in extra payments (the $100 you sent monthly), but also five years and two months, you will not spend $1,074/month, totaling more than $66,000.

Suppose you sell the house after five, ten, or fifteen years. How much a $100 a month would have saved you?

Impact of additional $100/month	Principal balance		Savings after deducting the extra payment
	With no additional payment	Paying additional $100/month	
After 5 years	$183,657	$176,857	$800
After 10 years	$162,684	$147,156	$3,528
After 15 years	$135,768	$109,039	$8,729

Every dollar counts, as every additional payment will be directed to the principal to pay off the debt. There are a few ways to make additional payments:

- You can send additional payments when possible.
- You can add a fixed amount to your monthly payments.
- You can pay your mortgage biweekly; make your mortgage payments every two weeks, resulting in an additional one monthly payment per year.

If the goal is to reduce the monthly payment as much as possible, there is no point in sending more money. You should consider this path to reduce the total interest paid or pay the mortgage faster without committing to the higher fixed monthly payment.

4. Putting your debt-ducks in a row.

You should investigate all your other debt in addition to the mortgage (e.g., credit cards, cars, etc.), as everything is considered when you apply for a mortgage. If you have an outstanding mortgage and pay other lenders very high-interest rates on cars or credit card repayment plans, you still pay large amounts in interest from your hard-earned money, and it does not benefit you. It does not matter who the lender is. Any improvement with one loan will allow you to pay the other loans faster.

Your debt impacts your finances in several ways:

- The actual interest paid to lenders
- Your ability to repay a mortgage
- Your mortgage qualification

You can take a few actions to check your current financial situation, and based on the findings, you can decide on the most convenient paths. Let's begin with a review of **key components:**

Debt-to-Income (DTI) ratio is the percentage of your monthly gross income that goes towards paying the minimum amount of your monthly debts.

Credit cards' credit limit is the maximum amount of credit a lender will extend to a debtor for a particular line of credit. What you owe on a credit card and the credit limit will determine the percentage of credit card usage. If you owe $400 and your credit limit is $1,000, your usage is 40%. The usage percentage will impact your credit score.

Minimum monthly payment is the least amount owed on a debt by a set due date without incurring penalties. The DTI will consider the loan's minimum monthly payments, and you need to be aware that if you make the minimum monthly payment on a credit card with high interest, it will take significant time to pay off that debt, and it will be very expensive.

A credit report is a borrower's credit history from several sources. Mortgage lenders review the credit report to determine the eligibility for a mortgage.

Credit bureaus: There are three credit bureaus; Experian, Equifax, and TransUnion. They provide **credit scores** and credit reports.

The first step will be to gather information about your debts using your credit reports and data from different creditors, such as credit cards or car loans.

You should review the actual interests you are paying on your debt. What are the credit limits, and what are your current interest rates? Some credit cards can have over 20% interest rate, and others can have a 0% introductory rate.

You should ask for a copy of your credit report from the three credit bureaus (Experian, Transunion, and Equifax) and add up all that is marked as balance and minimum payment. What is your total debt, and what is the monthly minimum payment amount? Use the following chart.

Debt	Credit limit	Balance	Interest rate	Monthly payment	Notes
Mortgage					
Car					
Car					
Credit Card					
Credit Card					
Credit Card					
Credit Card					
Other					
Other					
Other					
Other					
TOTAL					

Review what you can pay off or if it is convenient to take a short-term personal loan to pay off the higher interest rate payments. You can also roll over the balance of a high-interest credit card to a 0% interest credit card, as some companies will offer a 0% interest for a certain number of months when you open a new account with them. Be aware that paying off loans with other loans is not a solution; it is a means rather than an end. The purpose is to reduce the interest rate while focusing on paying down the loan. You will need to do the math on your monthly payments and calculate how long it will take you to pay off the loans.

Think and decide. What are your preferences?

- Do you want to pay the lowest total interest on your debt?
- Do you want to pay the least per month and focus on short-term goals?
- What is your monthly financial comfort level?

Preferences change with time, and it is important to re-evaluate your goals and your plans as time passes.

CHAPTER 3: SUMMARY

Total Mortgage Debt Cost
Total payments of Principal and Interest

DEBT COST

Impact Of Additional Payments
Reduces the mortgage term and the overall interest paid to the lender.

Term Of A Loan
Term in agreement vs. the term you plan paying

Overall Personal Debt
The total amount of your debt, such as a mortgage, car and credit cards.

As we focus on home ownership, remember that it is not a business disengaged from your personal finances. Make a plan to address your total debt, ensuring it is aligned to help position yourself to better qualify for your next mortgage. If needed, reduce your monthly payments or reduce the overall interest you pay lenders. Understand your numbers and make them work in your favor.

Rental Income

It was mid-September, and we had just moved a few months earlier to another rental in New Jersey. One day, while running errands, I got a call from my husband. He asked if I could arrive at the South Orange Animal Shelter to see the babies before he brought them home. Our old cat had died the previous month, and I suspected my husband would not wait long before bringing another pet home. "What do you mean babies, as in plural?" I asked, somewhat hesitantly.

My husband began emphasizing how concerned he was that, in the last few weeks, our older son had begun to be afraid of dogs, and even though there were no negative encounters with dogs, my son was very stressed if he was in a house where there was a dog. My husband continued, "I have the solution. It will either be a therapist for years or puppies now. Come see them!" Before hanging up, he added, "and Amir wanted a red and blue cat!"

I knew our daily routine would make it challenging to have a dog. On the other hand, I knew he was right. I did not know where that fear of dogs came from, and it had to be addressed. I knew exactly why my husband wanted me to meet him at the shelter; it is easy to fall in love with puppies.

As I entered the reception area of the animal shelter, a small round ball of hair ran towards me; an adorable little puppy full of energy. She was about six weeks old, with a contagious positive energy. She was blind in one eye, probably due to abuse, according to the vet. I looked for my husband, and there he was, standing next to a wall. He pointed at the ball of hair jumping around next to me while holding another puppy that looked like a small Labrador with light brown hair. He looked sad and did not want to walk. "They have one ginger cat," he said.

"Why?" I asked.

"Amir wanted a blue and a red cat, so this will be the red one."

I looked at the animals with mixed feelings, thinking of the loads of work they would create and how positive it would be on so many levels. That day, we returned home with the three babies.

After a few days, I spoke with my landlord about a minor repair that needed to be done on the kitchen sink. He was a very nice older man, and we often discussed other topics. Excited, I told him about the puppies. Quietly and slowly, he responded, "Orli, you can't have dogs. It is in the contract."

I was quiet. I felt frozen. I did not even think about it. I forgot about the limitation. It did not even cross my mind. Even though we had only had the puppies for a few days, I could not take them back. I did not want to. I had a long conversation with the landlord. I offered to add a deposit to assure him he had security in case of any damages, and I apologized lengthily. By the end of the conversation, the landlord accepted the solution with the deposit and additional pet fee.

Everything ended okay, but I had a bad feeling of "what if it wouldn't have ended that way?"

We had moved into that house a few months earlier because our former landlord was planning on selling the home where we had previously lived.

If you are renting for a while, you may have that feeling of "enough." You want your own space. You want to be able to decide on your own when to move, if you want to have minor changes in the home, or if you can have pets or not. You want to be able to decide for yourself.

Often, speaking with friends and clients that were renters and now landlords, we reflect on our own experiences as renters on the desire or lack of intention to be a landlord.

It is beneficial to isolate the emotional part of owning a rental property, regardless of whether you buy a single-family, live in the home and intend to rent it later when you move out, or buy a multi-family and live in one unit. If you buy a single-family and live there for a minimum of one year, it gives you time to know the ins and outs of the home, what repairs you should expect in the near future, what was already addressed, or what other challenges you can expect. It is also less intimidating than spending an additional large amount on an investment property.

House hacking refers to ways you can generate income from your home. If you buy a multi-family, two to four units, you can live in one unit and rent the other one to three units. In the next chapters, we will get more into the logistics when we learn about the property types from the financial perspective. I would like to focus on rental income from a wealth accumulation perspective, focusing on two aspects; rental income goals and revising if the rental income is sufficient to cover actual costs.

1. Rental income goals

We can speak lengthy about the approach towards having a rental income and what you feel about owning and living in a multi-family and renting out your other units to your neighbors or buying a single-family to rent it out in a year or two. If, for example, on an annual basis, you rent the property and end up with a $1,200 surplus, equivalent to $100 per month, is it worth your time and effort? To answer this, we need to go back to the goals. We will review three approaches:

- Home equity
- Passive income
- Home appreciation capital gain

If you end the year with a $1,200 surplus, does it mean you added $1,200 to your wealth? You actually added more than this amount. The equity, the actual cash value you have in the property, is the amount added to your wealth. Every month the debt is being paid off, and over time the property usually appreciates, so over time, even though you break even or have a small profit in your income and expenses balance, you increase your cash value. As in the first years of the mortgage, the payments go more to interest than principal, the wealth accumulation over a larger period of time will be much more significant than just a few years. There can be a significant market appreciation, but we do not rely on this; we estimate the average trend over time.

If you plan to retire in two years and would like to have a rental property to generate income, the scenario of an average of $100 a month will not fulfill this purpose. In this scenario, you can benefit from living in a multi-family if the budget shows you cover your expenses from the neighbors' rent and you do not have any expense of rent or out-of-pocket mortgage, including the property taxes, the home insurance, and home repairs if the expenses are paid by your neighbors.

Another scenario is if your area is increasing its value and there are indications for significant migration to the area and expected home value increases above the average appreciation over time. Some lenders will allow an interest-only mortgage, and this means two things: Your debt is not decreasing as you are paying monthly only the interest, and as a result of this, your monthly expense would be lower compared to if you would have paid monthly the principal and interest. In a few years, when the home appreciates to the amount you want to sell, you will cover the debt and benefit from the capital gain. This approach is not beneficial for long-term holding because if you plan to hold the property for twenty or thirty years, you probably should pay the mortgage off.

2. Is the rental income sufficient?

Do the math based on the current market and check if the rental income will cover part or all the expenses. You need to check it on a monthly and yearly basis.

What is the current expected income for this property? Consult your realtor and take vacancies into consideration. Estimate the monthly costs:

- Mortgage (principal, interest, and **mortgage insurance**, if relevant)
- Property taxes
- **Home insurance**
- **Home Owners Association** (HOA) fees, if relevant
- Water, sewer, and trash, if applicable

Set aside money for repairs, management costs (if managed by others), and other services if required, such as pest control, mechanic services for the A/C and furnace, or other repairs.

The result of this analysis will help you determine if this is a path you want to take with this specific property. The numbers can work well, and the income will cover the expenses. The income might cover most costs, but if the income margin is tight, you might have out-of-pocket expenses to hold this property. If you are comfortable with this because your property's debt is being paid down, that's okay. If you feel uncomfortable with the financial balance and want to hold the property, this might not be the right property to buy now. Do the math based on the current market, not future desires and hopes.

Do you want to manage a property you do not live in? This is a personal preferance. There is no right or wrong answer. I am just laying out some thoughts so you can decide your direction. Do you feel comfortable collecting the rent and getting calls from tenants? It can be a meeting scheduled ahead of time or an urgent maintenance problem in the middle of the night. When a tenant moves out, minor updates are usually needed before you put the property back on the market. New proposed tenants need to be screened, and lease agreements need to be signed. Are you willing to do this? If you hire a property manager, include this in your budget.

CHAPTER 4: SUMMARY

RENTAL INCOME

Rental Income
Can your Rental income
cover your expenses?

Rental Income goals
Passive income, lower debt, or
future home appreciation?

Keep the big picture in mind to determine if this path can benefit you. You might use it just once before you move to your desired forever home, or you can repeat this approach. The analysis will provide you guidance if the specific property, considering the market and the budget, is the right path to achieve your goal.

STEP 1 WORKSHEET

You will find questions to guide you in the compilation of information on your current situation, your goals, and preferences. At this initial step, do not expect to find a definite solution. The goal is to provide an array of options, clear questions, doubts, and map what additional information you need to gather.

General questions:

- What does wealth means to you?
- If wealth is defined by an amount of money, what is this number?
- If wealth is defined by a passive income, how much would you need per month?
- What are the life events you will consider as milestones that will require certain financial outcomes at that point?
- From reading these chapters, what aspect intrigues you to know further?
- Is there any approach that you feel is definitely not for you?

Primary residence:

- If you need to choose between your ideal property and your future financial goals for the next three years, what will prevail?
- Is multi-family a path you would like to explore?
- Would you consider selling your home for tax exempt profit?

Home Equity:

♦ Would you prefer to put down the lowest down payment or the highest possible amount?
♦ If you are looking to increase home equity:
  ◊ Are you planning on improving a property?
  ◊ Are you planning to wait and sell when the market will provide you with the desired profit?

Your Debt:

♦ Are you making unnecessary payments to lenders, paying high interest if that can be avoided?
♦ Is there room to improve your personal debt situation?

Rental Property:

♦ Would you like to be a landlord?
♦ Will you use a management company?

STEP 2
THE PROPERTY

"In every single thing you do, you are choosing a direction. Your life is a product of choices." – Dr. Kathleen Hall

Imagine you are with your realtor standing at the front door of a property you asked to preview, looking around as your realtor opens the lockbox on the doorknob. You love the neighborhood. You drove by so many times on your way to work. You have the feeling that maybe, just maybe, this is the one. You turn around as you hear the front door open.

Is this scenario familiar to you? The excitement of the search, touring the home, and imagining exactly how everything will fit in. The process can move very fast from this point onward. You make an offer, and if it is accepted, the clock begins ticking.

Before getting to this point, and way before you fall in love with a property, analyze your goals and priorities. Understanding your financial commitment before you start your search and the house-hunting journey will help you make better decisions. Should you listen to your brain or your heart?

Many clients I've worked with were looking to fall in love with a house. Sometimes, you do not want to focus on the longer-term benefits when you can move into your dream home in six to eight weeks. Others will be excited because they can visualize themselves achieving their long-term goals.

The property type, price, needs and wants, will be all on the checklist for your realtor to facilitate the search. The exit strategy is your property contingency plan. How long do you plan to hold onto the property, and would you sell it or rent it? Your exit strategy can impact the analysis to determine if a particular property is a correct purchase for you. If it is impossible to make this future decision at the current time, general guidance on your goals will work. There is a difference between your goals and your path, so as long as you set up your goals, your team will facilitate your search, and you will determine your path.

If your goal is financial, the search can vary, depending on if you are looking to maximize your financial gain or if you want to minimize your monthly cost. If your goal is the property, you want to ensure that it includes all your must-haves, and your search will be narrowed accordingly, considering your financial flexibility.

We cannot predict the future. With real estate, you can't know how the market will perform in several years. If the numbers do not work in the present-day market, you should not proceed. If your exit strategy is to rent the home in a few years, and in today's market, the rent does not cover the expenses and you do not want to add money monthly, or if you plan to cash out equity based on the home's future appreciation without a plan on investing in the property, the house at that price might not be compatible with your goals.

While reading through the next three chapters, create three lists, one per chapter, describing your ideal goals or needs regarding that chapter's topic. When done, review if the lists match. For example, you might wish for a multi-family to get rental income from the beginning, but the neighborhood you like has just single-family homes. You might wish to live on a single-family ranch, and you do not like the idea of needing to move. If there is any discrepancy between your lists, hold on to it as your planning journey continues, and let's begin.

STEP 2 includes:

Chapter 5:
Needs & Wants

Chapter 6:
Property Type

Chapter 7:
Exit Strategy

The Needs and Wants

Outline your must-haves, deal breakers, and preferences in your ideal home checklist. For some, a school district or a first-floor bedroom can be a deal breaker. For others, it can be the layout, the home's condition, if it is move-in ready, or if it has the desired fixtures. If you do not plan to reside in the house by yourself, it is crucial to account for the preferences of all parties involved.

When I designed single-family homes, clients often commented that coming to us was like going to couples' therapy. Before the initial design stage, when we generally spoke about the checklist, it often looked like the couple agreed upon what they wanted, some items were a joint desire, and each added a few more wants or needs to the list. Differences would surface when the actual design progressed, as budget and square footage were limited. Solutions are possible, but sometimes it requires more work or compromises.

Let me share one of my experiences in this matter; it is a story about my submarine. Yes, I had one. At least, that is how my kids described my bedroom. We decided to buy a house in Millburn, New Jersey. The average cost of homes was high, but we were very interested in the school district. We decided to buy a home that needed some love and renovations, rehab the house, and sell it for a profit after we moved on. We found a house within walking distance of schools, the park, and the commuter train to NYC. We renovated the kitchen and bathrooms, and enclosed a porch next to the kitchen. To accommodate the number of bedrooms, we decided to convert the sunroom on the first floor into our bedroom. The room was 20' x 7', with windows all around. During the renovations, we added a large closet from the adjoining family room space. It was minimalistic and lovely, and the curtains were closed most of the time because there were windows all around. Any time my kids would refer to our bedroom, they would refer to it as "the submarine." This accommodation allowed us to get other benefits from this home.

Here are some aspects to consider, and feel free to add more to the list:

- ◆ Location:
  - ◊ Neighborhood
  - ◊ Town
  - ◊ School zone
  - ◊ Driving time to a certain location

- ◆ Home desires or needs:
  - ◊ Number of bedrooms and bathrooms
  - ◊ Specific bedroom and bathroom requirements (more or less privacy, sizes of closets and bathrooms, floor level)
  - ◊ Home office
  - ◊ Laundry room
  - ◊ Mudroom
  - ◊ Kitchen size and condition
  - ◊ Pantry
  - ◊ Basement
  - ◊ Family Room
  - ◊ Yard

♦   Move-in ready, minor cosmetic repairs, or a rehab. The idea of rehabbing the home you are moving into can sound fascinating. Some (like my husband) feel the opposite and would prefer to purchase a home that doesn't require renovations. What is your comfort level?

There are different levels of repairs, updates, or renovations needed; each comes with a price tag of the actual cost of time and money and the comfort level associated with each. Some repairs will require a minimum determined time frame, most work will be done by professionals, and you need to allocate the time and budget, hopefully, all to be done before you move in, such as paint, carpet, or maybe windows or a fence.

A dated house will cost less than a recently renovated home. If you plan on buying a dated home and renovating it, there are a few steps to consider. You should compare the home purchase and renovation costs to the market value of a comparable home in the level of finish you aspire to get in your renovation. The goal is that the sum of the renovation cost plus the house's original price will be less than the market value after renovations. You might opt for sweat equity and do some of the upgrades yourself.

After you narrow your search to comply with your needs and wants, be aware of the home's up-front potential. Some properties, dated or not, show their potential very quickly. You can see and feel the flow, the natural light, and the ceiling heights. The house might be in mint condition, or some areas might benefit from an update; however, it is easy to use your imagination for potential improvements. With others, it can be more challenging, especially if there is a disturbing smell, as it often happens when a place has been closed up for too long or if it has outdated wallpaper combined with other dated elements. It can easily disrupt one's view of the potential in the home.

When brainstorming your list in advance, you should be clear about your dealbreakers, must-haves, and what can be negotiated regarding existing fixtures and the home's condition. A Japanese proverb says, "Vision without action is a daydream. Action without vision is a nightmare."

When you take action, you need to ensure that it supports your vision.

CHAPTER 5: SUMMARY

Condition
Move-in ready, cosmetic repairs or rehab.

Location

Physical characteristics
Size, number of bedrooms, other.

Property Type

We will review the property types under the eyes of mortgage qualifications and financial impact. You know your personal preferences, so the goal of this chapter is to provide further information for you to consider.

If you prefer to live in a condominium, consider HOA expenses and by-laws limitations, as they can impact your budget, mortgage qualifications, future rental, and more. When looking for the cost of the monthly HOA, check what it includes. Sometimes it only includes common areas and some service expenses, as physical elements of the building and building's insurance. The HOA can also cover some utilities, such as water, sewer, and more. If two condominiums charge the same HOA monthly amount, while one covers some utilities and the other does not, it will impact your monthly budget differently.

If you plan on having a government loan, such as FHA or VA, be aware that both agencies have lists of approved condominiums. Those agencies will approve your mortgage only if the property is on their list. You might plan on asking for a VA loan with no money down, and even though you comply with the mortgage requirements, if the condo is not marked as a current approved condo on the government agency list, the application will be rejected. All the lists are public information on the agencies websites. The government agencies do not have approved list limitations on single-family homes, but rather requirements on the condition of the homes, such as the need to be in good, safe, and operating conditions. Conventional loans do not have the requirements of approved lists.

If a multi-family property is not your cup of tea, proceed with the other options. If a multi-family property is a good option, or you are not sure yet, use the following comparison regarding the cost of the property and mortgage implications as additional perspectives.

Cost of a property

If a multi-family property is more expensive than a single-family, review the following:

- Can you still qualify for the higher purchase price?
- Can a longer mortgage term help you qualify for the mortgage?
- Can you afford the monthly payments? Will it cost you more out of pocket after considering the rental income?

Multi-family can cost you less monthly out of pocket, and a realtor can guide you regarding the actual revenue potential and expenses of properties in your desired area.

SCENARIO ANALYSIS—COMPARING PROPERTY COSTS

How much will a property cost you monthly? Let's assume you are looking at two properties: a single-family listed at $400,000 where you will pay the full mortgage monthly payment out of pocket, and a quadruplex listed at $600,000. In both scenarios, you will pay a $60,000 down payment. Looking at the mortgage P&I, taxes, and insurance, how much will it cost you monthly? There can be additional mortgage insurance, pending the loan program chosen and the loan amount. This exercise aims to understand the potential and the two different approaches.

	Single family	**Quadruplex**	
Purchase price	$400,000	$600,000	
Down Payment	$60,000	$60,000	
Mortgage amount	$340,000	$540,000	
Taxes (yearly)	$4,500	$7,200	Estimated
Insurance (yearly)	$1,800	$2,400	Estimated
Rent income (per unit)	$0	$1,200	Estimated, per unit

Estimated monthly payment for a 30-year loan at 5%:

*Taxes and home insurance are estimations only.
Additional mortgage insurance is not calculated.

	Single family	Quadruplex	
P&I	$1,825	$2,899	
Taxes	$375	$600	
Insurance	$150	$200	
Other	$0	$200	
Expense	$2,350	$3,899	
Income	$0	$3,600	Excluding vacancies

Mortgage implications

If you plan to live in the multi-family property for a few years, keep it, rent it, and move on, there are other aspects to consider in advance to ensure you can execute your plans, such as your future down payment for the next property and your next mortgage qualifications.

Estimate how much you need to save every month to ensure you have the down payment when the time comes. Yes, you can plan on having your next mortgage with a minimum down payment, but you still need the money. There is an option that your property will appreciate in two or three years, and you will be able to refinance, cashing out on the equity and keeping the money for the down payment of your next home purchase. This is a great option when possible, but you can only rely on this if you did major renovations that increased the home's value.

Another aspect you need to consider is your future mortgage qualifications to be approved to purchase your next property. The lender will calculate your total income and your total expenses.

If you own a single-family and plan to put it on the market after you purchase your next home, your total debt will include your current and next mortgages. Your income will remain the same, as you did not rent your current home before closing on your next home. Check with your lender to learn if you can qualify with a mortgage program that allows a higher debt ratio. You can always refinance after you move out and rent the previous home, taking into consideration the mortgage program and lender's requirements. Some lenders will accept a signed lease on your current home, on or before the closing of your future property, to include the rental income and lower your DTI, and other lenders will accept only the rent income reported on Schedule E in your taxes.

If you are purchasing a multi-family property with current renters in some of the units, some lenders will require the lease agreement to calculate the income, and others as mentioned, will not accept that unless reported in your taxes, which means you cannot have the rental income considered in the DTI when purchasing the property.

Know your market

The wish for a particular property might be unrealistic in a specific market at the price range that you want or in the area that you desire, but it might be a perfect match in another market or another state. The housing market varies significantly over the years, based on location. Your options in New York City, St. Louis, Missouri, and West Orange, New Jersey, are vastly different.

We spoke about the goals and the theoretically ideal property to achieve these goals; however, every market will present different opportunities.

Learn your market. What are the possibilities? What is the inventory? Is your location flexible or will the property be based on availability in a particular area?

Your realtor can provide valuable information, and you can use multiple public data resources to learn about the trends of migration and forecasts, as in the following publication of Freddie Mac.

Freddie Mac is a federal home loan mortgage corporation, and in June of 2022, they published a research titled, "In pursuit of affordable housing: the migration of homebuyers within the US; before and after the pandemic.[1] "They listed the top ten cities affected by the net migration and the median home prices sold and purchased in those locations.

1. "In Pursuit of Affordable Housing: The Migration of Homebuyers within the U.S.-before and after the Pandemic," Freddie Mac, accessed January 22, 2023, https://www.freddiemac.com/research/insight/20220622-pursuit-affordable-housing-migration-homebuyers-within.

Home prices in the top 10 destination metro areas gaining the most homebuyers vs. their metro areas of origin

On average, the median price of a home in these metro areas was $128,000 less than the median home price in their top metro of origin.

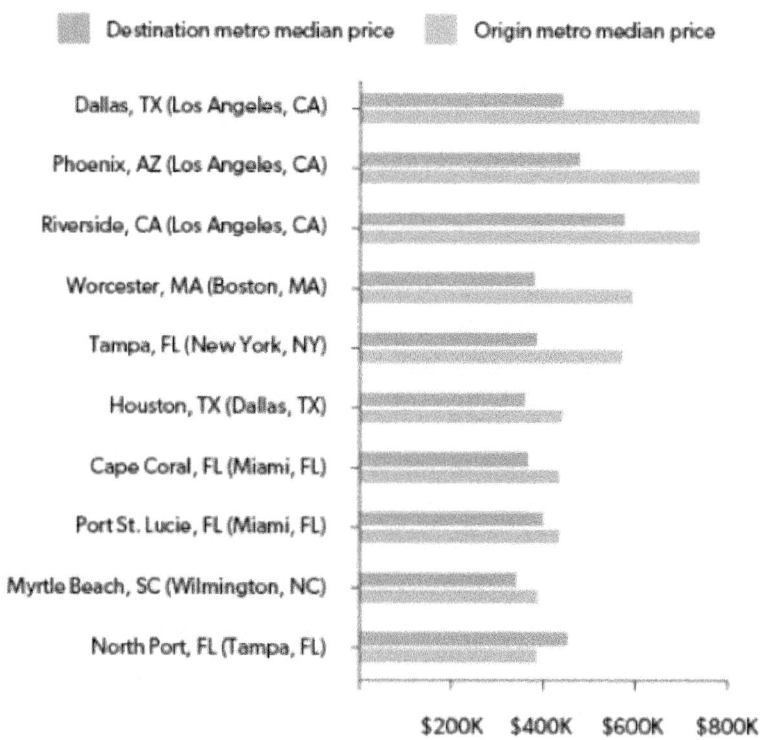

Home prices in the top 10 metro areas of origin losing the most homebuyers vs. their destination metro areas

On average, the median price of a home in these metro areas was $144,000 more than the median home price in their top metro destination.

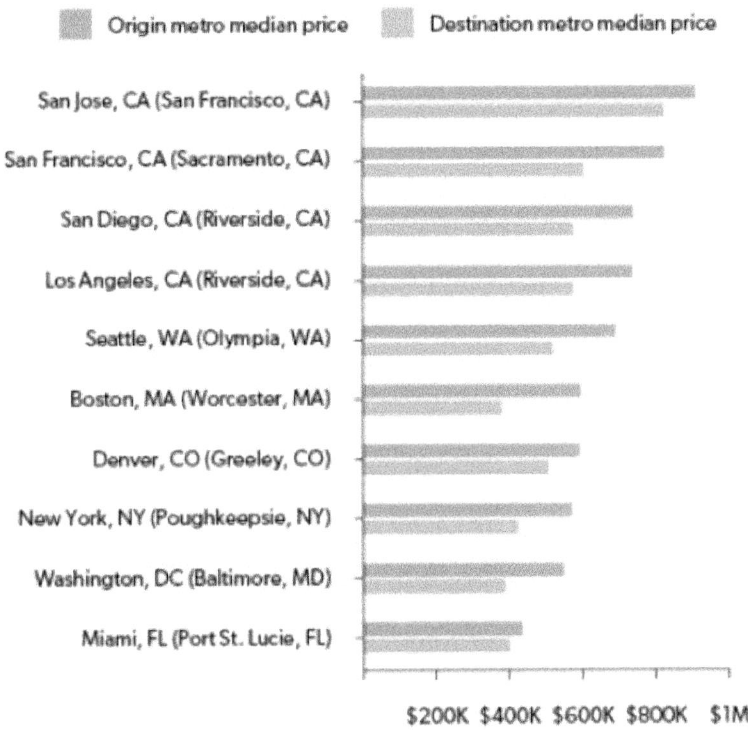

Top metro areas ranked by homebuyer net migration March 2020 – February 2022

Net migration was highest in affordable interior markets, New England regions and Florida.

Rank	Metro area	Net migration Mar 2020 – Feb 2022	Net migration Mar 2018 – Feb 2020
1	Riverside-San Bernardino-Ontario, CA	17,339	5,300
2	Worcester, MA-CT	5,934	1,187
3	North Port-Sarasota-Bradenton, FL	5,741	1,743
4	Phoenix-Mesa-Chandler, AZ	5,422	4,780
5	Myrtle Beach-Conway-North Myrtle Beach, SC-NC	5,197	2,094
6	Tampa-St. Petersburg-Clearwater, FL	5,176	2,173
7	Cape Coral-Fort Myers, FL	4,872	1,226
8	Port St. Lucie, FL	4,826	1,385
9	Dallas-Fort Worth-Arlington, TX	4,781	1,477
10	Houston-The Woodlands-Sugar Land, TX	4,340	879
11	Deltona-Daytona Beach-Ormond Beach, FL	4,262	1,643
12	Lakeland-Winter Haven, FL	4,070	1,640
13	Las Vegas-Henderson-Paradise, NV	4,046	1,471
14	Sacramento-Roseville-Folsom, CA	3,783	1,610
15	Greeley, CO	3,732	1,734
16	Jacksonville, FL	3,434	1,536
17	Salisbury, MD-DE	3,308	1,128
18	Poughkeepsie-Newburgh-Middletown, NY	3,200	1,297
19	Stockton, CA	2,768	894
20	Columbia, SC	2,662	719
21	Palm Bay-Melbourne-Titusville, FL	2,507	957
22	Ocala, FL	2,325	1,075
23	Boise City, ID	2,292	1,450
24	Hartford-East Hartford-Middletown, CT	**2,188**	**185**
25	Punta Gorda, FL	2,182	803
26	Allentown-Bethlehem-Easton, PA-NJ	1,921	470
27	San Antonio-New Braunfels, TX	1,909	859
28	Spartanburg, SC	1,791	870
29	Bridgeport-Stamford-Norwalk, CT	1,785	424
30	New Haven-Milford, CT	**1,654**	**70**
31	Tucson, AZ	1,638	1,035
32	Richmond, VA	1,609	819
33	Bakersfield, CA	**1,594**	**268**
34	York-Hanover, PA	1,567	427
35	Hagerstown-Martinsburg, MD-WV	1,506	684

Rank	Metro area	Net migration Mar 2020 – Feb 2022	Net migration Mar 2018 – Feb 2020
1	New York-Newark-Jersey City, NY-NJ-PA	-49,880	-16,095
2	Los Angeles-Long Beach-Anaheim, CA	-47,571	-16,330
3	San Francisco-Oakland-Berkeley, CA	-25,061	-8,379
4	Washington-Arlington-Alexandria, DC-VA-MD-WV	-20,773	-6,777
5	San Jose-Sunnyvale-Santa Clara, CA	-15,692	-5,665
6	Boston-Cambridge-Newton, MA-NH	-15,039	-5,887
7	Seattle-Tacoma-Bellevue, WA	-11,952	-3,957
8	San Diego-Chula Vista-Carlsbad, CA	-6,592	-2,987
9	Miami-Fort Lauderdale-Pompano Beach, FL	-6,492	-3,259
10	Denver-Aurora-Lakewood, CO	-6,264	-1,976
11	Chicago-Naperville-Elgin, IL-IN-WI	-6,131	-4,515
12	Portland-Vancouver-Hillsboro, OR-WA	-3,826	-1,163
13	Minneapolis-St. Paul-Bloomington, MN-WI	-3,177	-1,248
14	Salt Lake City, UT	-3,108	-1,381
15	Boulder, CO	-2,793	-1,385
16	Detroit-Warren-Dearborn, MI	-2,304	-1,003
17	Providence-Warwick, RI-MA	**-1,844**	**127**
18	Urban Honolulu, HI	-1,626	-980
19	Columbus, OH	-1,438	-413
20	Milwaukee-Waukesha, WI	-1,197	-536
21	New Orleans-Metairie, LA	-976	-195
22	Louisville/Jefferson County, KY-IN	-968	-85
23	Philadelphia-Camden-Wilmington, PA-NJ-DE-MD	-879	-416
24	Madison, WI	-789	-370
25	Santa Maria-Santa Barbara, CA	-733	-219
26	Buffalo-Cheektowaga, NY	-728	-256
27	Ann Arbor, MI	-725	-569
28	Salinas, CA	-653	-212
29	Cincinnati, OH-KY-IN	**-642**	**587**
30	Santa Cruz-Watsonville, CA	-621	-174
31	Lexington-Fayette, KY	-556	-195
32	Nashville-Davidson--Murfreesboro--Franklin, TN	-536	-39
33	Memphis, TN-MS-AR	-514	-209
34	Pittsburgh, PA	**-491**	**59**
35	Rochester, NY	-467	-118

Note: Highlighted metro areas saw more than a tenfold change in homebuyer net migration in the two years occurring before and after the start of the pandemic.

Source: Freddie Mac Loan Product Advisor®

CHAPTER 6: SUMMARY

PROPERTY TYPE

Cost of a Property
Single-family vs.
Multi Family.

Mortgage
Impact of a rental
on your
Debt-To-Income
(DTI)

Property Type
Single Family,
apartment,
townhome,
or up to four
units multifamily.

Reality Check
What are the
options in your
market

Exit Strategy

The exit strategy is the contingency plan you have for the property. You could plan to keep the home and rent it, sell it for a profit, keep the house and pass it on to a family member, and more. Each direction will impact the initial analysis when considering whether you should buy the property.

Sometimes, it is challenging to elaborate on an exit strategy when all you want to do now is buy a home. The effort required to make the decision and elaborate the logistics to purchase and move to your new home can push aside long-term plans. If you fall in love with your soon to be your new home, the exit strategy can be pushed even further if the current plan does not match your long-term goals. This is fine; as long as you are aware of this, you are conscious of your decisions and their impact.

Let's review two options: selling and renting.

When you buy a property with the intent to sell it in the future for financial gain, you will analyze the potential based on the price of the property you are currently buying. Do you plan to do renovations that will increase the home's value, or are you paying the principal down aggressively?

When you plan on renting the property after you move out, it is important to check that the income can cover the expenses and to know how you will qualify for your next property, even if you plan to do that five years later. By planning, you can find solutions that will not be possible at the last moment when you are ready to move out.

It is convenient to have the plan on paper and re-evaluate the options every year or two, review aspects that can help you position yourself better financially in the immediate present and can put you in a better position when executing your exit strategy.

An objective theoretical brainstorming on your goals, and how to use your exit strategy to achieve those goals, is very different from the emotional involvement when you review your options while living in the house. Can you analyze your priorities objectively? Often, translating each option to numbers, helps make a decision. How much you gain, how much you spend, how will those profits, savings or expenses impact other aspects of your life? Follow the numbers, and in any given time, by honest with yourself.

SCENARIO ANALYSIS:
CALCULATING CAPITAL GAIN

Let's assume you bought a property at $250,000 with 20% down; your mortgage was $200,000. You took a 30 year mortgage at 5% and sold the property five years later at $285,000.

In this scenario, from the $285,000 sale price, we will deduct $183,657, the debt after five years, if you did not make extra payments. This would leave you with $101,343 less the closing expenses, such as the realtor's fee, and repairs expenses. Remember, in this scenario, you invested the initial $50,000, and the profit is $51,343, less any expenses.

CHAPTER 7: SUMMARY

Selling the property
Benefit from tax-exempt capital gain.

Renting the property
Investment property, rent, and increase the equity.

STEP 2 WORKSHEET

If you currently own a home
- ◆ Location:
    - ◊ Where do you live?
    - ◊ Is it an appreciating market? Do the properties in your area increase their value?

- ◆ Property type and fit:
    - ◊ What type of home do you own?
    - ◊ When did you buy the property?
    - ◊ For how long do you plan on staying at this home?
    - ◊ If you are planning to move in the future, why?

- ◆ Property value:
    - ◊ What is the current home market value?
    - ◊ How much is your home debt balance?
    - ◊ How much is your home equity value?

- ◆ Current mortgage:
    - ◊ Did you refinance since purchasing your home?
    - ◊ What mortgage do you have? Conventional / FHA / VA / USDA
    - ◊ What is your loan term?
    - ◊ What is your loan interest rate?
    - ◊ Do you pay mortgage insurance?
    - ◊ Do you escrow?
    - ◊ What is your monthly payment?
    - ◊ Do you pay any additional payments?

- ◆ Mortgage's goals:
    - ◊ Pay less per month?
    - ◊ Pay off the mortgage faster? Any specific time frame?
    - ◊ Refinance cash out from the home equity? If yes, how much money and for what purpose?

If you are currently renting
- ◆ Lease agreement
  - ◊ When does the lease end?
  - ◊ How much advance notice do you need to provide?
  - ◊ If needed, can you renew your lease agreement on a monthly basis?
  - ◊ How much do you pay rent per month?
  - ◊ How much did you pay for rent in the last twelve months?
- ◆ Home ownership
  - ◊ Did you previously own a home?
  - ◊ Would you like to buy a home?
  - ◊ If you do, what holds you back?

Information on your future home
- ◆ What will be your property's location?
  - ◊ Neighborhood / town / school zone / driving time to a particular location.
  - ◊ From the above, what is a must and what is desired?
- ◆ What are your property checklist needs and wants?
  - ◊ What is a must-have?
  - ◊ What would you like to have, but it is not a deal breaker?
    - Priority 1:
    - Priority 2:
    - Priority 3:
  - ◊ Any general information as to floor plan style you prefer?
- ◆ Property condition
  - ◊ Do you have a clear preference for move-in ready, minor cosmetic repairs, or a rehab?
  - ◊ What are your deal breakers?
  - ◊ Balancing property condition and financial gain, what prevails?
- ◆ What property type would you like?
  - ◊ Single-family or multi-family?
- ◆ Your exit strategy: are you interested in house hacking?
  - ◊ If yes, one time or multiple times?

STEP 3
FINANCING

"People buy on emotion and justify on logic." —Zig Ziglar

Buying on emotion and justifying on logic, in large-scale decisions, can put us in situations we would prefer to avoid, regardless of how far we go to justify it. It is nice to daydream about your ideal home, and it should be even better when you purchase the home you fell in love with. The reality of your actions can go both ways. You might have made a very prosperous financial decision or taken one that will lead you to a financial constraint. When making decisions so impactful to your financial future, do not leave it to luck or arbitrary outcome, deriving from feeling excited and accomplished for a limited time at the initial part of your home ownership journey.

In the following five chapters, you will learn about the finances of a mortgage. Why do you need to understand the process in detail? How can we simplify this, and what should you expect from the process? Let me paint you a picture of a scenario that happened to me many times while working as a mortgage loan officer (MLO).

I received a phone call mid-morning; a client was unsure if he wanted to refinance and wanted to check his options. We reviewed why he would be interested in refinancing, and often it is to reduce the monthly payment, pay the mortgage faster, or do a cash-out refinance to consolidate debt or have cash on hand. By understanding the client's goals, I can provide better solutions. I gathered personal information, ran a credit check, reviewed any questions that may arise, and proceeded with more details about the property and the income. About ten to fifteen minutes into the call, I began working on the different mortgage options. At the same time, the client often takes advantage of the time and gathers some needed income documentation. Soon after, I shared with the client his options, the program, the terms, monthly payments, the cost of the loan, and all the other relevant information. We compared the different programs as needed, and about an hour after the conversation began, the client chose his preferred program. I can lock in the interest rate. We reviewed all the documentation, the loan application was signed, the documents were submitted, and the application could begin the process on the same day. An appraisal could be ordered, and if we got an appraisal waiver, the closing could happen in a week or two. As simple as that.

If the process can be simple, why do you need to understand the process and pay attention to the details? Because it is not always straightforward, some options are not always in your favor, and the MLO provides a solution based on your present conditions. You do not know what you do not know, what you should or could have done. Understanding mortgage finances will allow you to work better with your mortgage loan officer, maximize the opportunities in the market, avoid costly mistakes, and achieve your financial goals.

The first chapter focused on the big picture, the direction, approaches, and possibilities. It is time to zoom in and unveil more detailed information. Learn about the types of mortgages available, the interest rate options and their impact, how the monthly payment structure will affect your wealth, and what you need to qualify for the mortgage of your choice. Learning early on what can benefit you provides you the time to implement needed changes or avoid actions that can harm you, making the difference between approval or rejection of a mortgage.

I want to share with you the impact of one action; the story of a client who **co-signed** a loan and the importance of the way the debt payments are made. A while ago, I spoke with a lady interested in refinancing for much-needed debt consolidation and lowering her monthly payment, as she was already late in her mortgage payments. Her Debt-to-Income (DTI) was too high, and the best option was to exclude from her debt calculations two debts she co-signed for her grandson, as he made the monthly payments. By excluding the debts, the DTI was lowered enough to qualify her under the FHA loan terms. All she needed was proof that her grandson was making the monthly payments. She could achieve that by providing the grandson's twelve months' bank statements, showing the monthly debt payments were being paid from that account and proving that she was not on the account. The grandson did not feel comfortable providing the information due to privacy matters. It took a significant amount of time until the grandmother convinced her grandson to provide the information, despite being aware that time was of the essence. When the grandson finally agreed and provided the information, the grandmother entered a new month of past due payment, exceeding the limits allowed by the FHA rules, and the application was rejected.

It is never too early to know what you need, the parameters by which you will be qualified for a mortgage, and what actions to avoid.

STEP 3 includes:

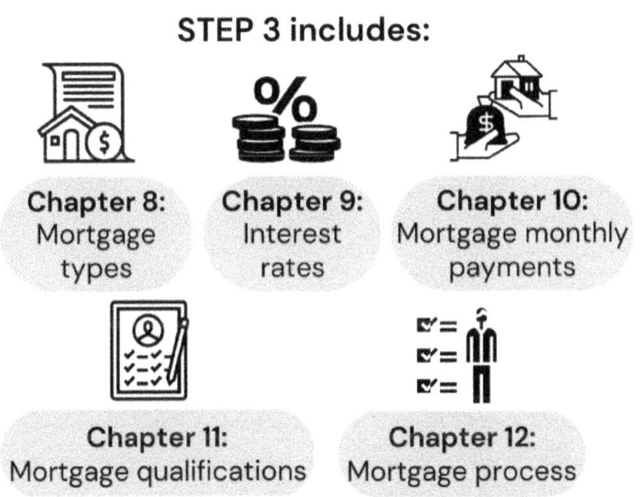

Mortgage Types

Mortgages in the market reflect different eligibility terms, advantages, and costs. Some loans are for targeted groups, such as eligible veterans or residents in rural developments with a limited income. Other loans are open to all, and you need to qualify under the loan terms.

Government loans are guaranteed by a government agency, which means that if the borrower defaults on his mortgage, the government agency will repay the lender. You apply for a government loan directly through a private lender that offers the mortgage type you want (with some exceptions in USDA loans). Each lender can set up additional program requirements, such as a higher credit score or a lower DTI, over and above the government agency's requirements.

There are three government-insured or backed mortgage loans: Veterans Administration (VA), US Department of Agriculture (USDA), and Federal Housing Administration (FHA). They generally provide better interest rates, and all have easier personal qualification criteria, as they allow a lower credit score and a higher DTI in addition to low or no down payment. The lower interest rates do not always reflect a lower monthly payment, as some loans have additional costs added to the principal debt or additional monthly expenses.

The government loans can be stricter in the property's qualifications, assuring the house's safety and proper condition. Government mortgages are available for primary residences only. You cannot qualify for a government loan when purchasing a second home or investment property.

- A **VA** loan is a government-guaranteed loan that facilitates home financing for eligible veterans and select surviving spouses. It allows the purchase of a home with no money down, a lower credit score, and compliance with outlined criteria; you can have a higher DTI and refinance up to 100% loan-to-value (LTV). The VA charges a VA funding fee as a one-time fee paid to the Department of Veterans, and you can roll this fee into the loan. There are eligibility criteria where the funding fee can be waived or reduced.
- An **FHA** loan is a US Federal Housing Administration-insured loan. You can qualify with a down payment as low as 3.5%. It allows a higher DTI (compared to a conventional loan), and has less restrictive credit score requirements. The FHA loan charges a **mortgage insurance premium** (MIP), which entails two charges:

  ◊ Up-front mortgage insurance is a charge when you issue the loan, which is paid to the Federal Housing Administration.
  ◊ A monthly mortgage insurance payment is charged in addition to your mortgage P&I, property taxes, and home insurance.

- A **USDA** loan is a government-backed loan that facilitates home financing for purchasing a primary residence in qualifying rural areas. It allows the purchase of a home with no money down.
- A **conventional loan** is any mortgage loan not guaranteed or insured by the government. Fannie Mae and Freddie Mac are government-sponsored enterprises that buy mortgages from lenders, and the lenders need to meet their required criteria, such as credit score and loan amount limits.

◊ Conventional conforming loans comply with Fannie Mae and Freddie Mac's requirements.

◊ Conventional nonconforming loans do not comply with Fannie Mae's or Freddie Mac's requirements, such as the **jumbo loan**, when the loan amount exceeds the conforming loan limits.

Let's simplify what we know thus far. There are two target group loans, the VA and the USDA. If you belong to either of these groups, you are also eligible to apply for the other mortgage programs. Other popular loans are FHA and conventional.

If you are planning on buying a condo, remember the VA and FHA agencies have approved lists for condominiums. This means that in order to approve a purchase or refinance loan for a condo, the lender will review the public records to check if the condo is on the approved list. If your condo is not on the list, or it is on the list and the term of the approval is expired, the FHA or VA loans will not be approved. Sometimes, you could have been approved for a condo in a VA or FHA loan a few years ago, and when you want to refinance, the condo approval term expired, so you will not be eligible to refinance a new FHA or VA loans unless you do VA IRRRL loan (Interest Rate Reduction Refinance Loan), an FHA Streamline Refinance program, complying with those additional loan guidelines, or change to a conventional loan, which has no restrictions on a condo.

Other significant preferences will be determined by the required down payment, eligibility criteria that is more comfortable for you, the interest rate offered, and the impact of additional charges as mortgage insurance.

Mortgage Insurance

Mortgage insurance lowers the risk to the lender for making a loan to you so that you can qualify for a loan that you might not otherwise be able to get. It increases the monthly cost of your loan, and it will be included in your total monthly payment to your lender.

In a conventional loan, you are required to pay **private mortgage insurance** (PMI) if your down payment is less than 20%. A **mortgage insurance premium** (MIP) is required on FHA loans, regardless of your down payment.

The significant difference between a PMI and MIP is the length of time you will pay this extra payment. In a conventional loan, the PMI will drop once you get under 78% LTV. In an FHA loan, if your down payment is 3.5%-10%, you will pay the MIP for the life of the loan. If your down payment exceeds 10%, you will pay the MIP for a set number of years.

For example, if a MIP is 0.85% of your debt in a $200,000 loan (On a $210,000 home purchase), you will pay $141 per month. If, after five years, the value of the home increases and you owe less than 80% of the home's value, you will continue paying the monthly payment of $141 MIP until the mortgage is paid off or you refinance.

Do not assume a loan is less convenient because you have the additional payment of mortgage insurance. As often the FHA has better interest rates than the conventional loan, do you really pay more per month, and how much?

In the example of the $200,000 loan mentioned above, let's compare the monthly cost if you can get a conventional 30-year loan at 5% and no PMI compared to an FHA 30-year loan at 4% and with MIP.

Conventional:
$1,074/month
FHA:
$955 + $141 = $1,096/month

You will pay $22 more per month by using the FHA loan, and due to the other more convenient FHA criteria, it can make all the difference between the mortgage being approved or not.

Loan-to-Value (LTV)

LTV determines the loan amounts possible. It is the percentage between the mortgage amount and the home's value. An **appraisal** provides the home's value. For example, if the mortgage amount is $280,000 and the home's value is $400,000, the LTV is 70%. LTV is reflected in different aspects of the loan:

- In a home purchase, you define the amount of down payment and the cash you need to bring to closing as a percentage of the home's value. If you can borrow 95% of the purchase amount, you will need to bring the remaining 5% and the closing costs to closing.
- If you want to refinance your mortgage and **cash out** some money to pay off debt or for any other purpose, most of the mortgage plans will limit the cash out to be maximum of 80% LTV from the appraised value of the home or 75% if the property is an investment. A cash-out refinance of your current home's loan with a bigger mortgage allows you to take advantage of your home's equity (cash value). The new mortgage will cover the existing mortgage debt, the cost of the new mortgage origination, and the cash you will get. If the appraised home's value is $380,000, the maximum new mortgage amount (in most cases) is 80%. This means the maximum new loan will be $304,000. If your current debt is $250,000 and the closing costs of the new loan are $4,000, the maximum cash you can get is $50,000.
- Based on your credit score, if it is on the lower end, you might refinance and be limited to a maximum loan amount of 75% LTV or lower.

You can estimate the home's value when you speak with the MLO, and as part of purchasing a home or refinancing a mortgage, the lender will order an appraisal of the home, and in some cases, the home appraisal can be waived. The appraisal result can be precise as estimated initially, higher or lower than the assessed value, and the options might be revised. Today, many websites offer home value estimates. I personally prefer working with Zillow.com. It uses an algorithm that calculates the home's value based on other information online, such as the sale price of other properties, the square footage of the house, and other factors. If the home has unique features, is renovated at a very high end, or is dated more than the average in the area, the actual value will differ from the one presented online. The prices online are often close to the actual range, and it can give you a general idea.

CHAPTER 8: SUMMARY

MORTGAGE TYPES

Conventional
Fixed or variable interest rate.
Pay PMI if the down payment is <20%

FHA
Requires MIP.
Minimum 3.5% down payment.
Less restrictive requirements.

VA
Requires VA Funding Fee. Can be $0 down payment.
Less restrictive requirements.

USDA
Geographical and financial requirements.
Can be $0 down payment.

 **Takeaways:**

- There are many more programs, including options for assistance with the down payments. When approaching an MLO, keep an open mind to hear and gather information on your options.
- You might often have an idea of what is beneficial or not based on a friend's experience or by comparing it to another person's solution. However, that might not be the best option for you. Only you know what you need. Only you know what you want. It is not always aligned with the other person's needs and wants.
- In the last few years, many lenders allowed borrowers to request a forbearance to pause or reduce payments for a limited time, and then negotiate with the lender the terms to repay the amount required. While it is a lifesaving solution in the short term, it impacts the immediate mortgage options available if you want to refinance after you come out of forbearance.

Interest Rates

find interest rates to be a fascinating topic. Yes, seriously. Usually, as consumers, we focus on the interest rate number, and many borrowers prefer the lowest possible fixed interest rates. I look at this from a different perspective, simply because those options are not in a vacuum. Each option has a price tag. Looking at your unique situation, you have to determine what will be the most convenient for you and how your loan cost spending can be targeted to achieve your desired goals. Having my husband's approach in mind, I will be precise in concepts and ideas and depict more in-depth information.

In a loan, the interest rate defines the cost of borrowing. The total cost of a loan includes the interest rate and origination charges. The interest rate is a percentage calculated annually, even though it is charged monthly, calculating the interest on the remaining principal amount. Understanding this concept will help you understand the **amortization** of a loan and your mortgage monthly payments.

A loan **amortization schedule** shows the complete chart of a loan's periodic payments, showing the amount of principal and interest that comprise each level of payment until the loan is paid off at the end of its term. Loan amortization tables can help borrowers track what they owe and forecast the outstanding balance or interest at any point in the cycle.

As the interest rate is calculated annually and charged monthly, if you have a $96,000 loan with a 5% interest rate, the first month's interest rate will be calculated as follows:

5% of $96,000 = $4,800 (annual charge)
$4,800 / 12 months = $400

The cost of the first-month interest is $400, but it does not determine your total monthly payment to repay the loan. When you pay $400 in the first month, your debt remains $96,000. A fully amortized loan means that if you make every payment according to the amortization schedule on your term loan, your loan will be fully paid off by the end of the term. If a loan is not fully amortized, you will owe the lender money by the end of the loan's term. We use fully amortized loans in this book's loan calculations and examples.

The additional monthly principal payment will be determined based on how much time you have to repay the loan. For example, if the loan above is calculated to be paid off in ten years, you will pay the first month $1,018, divided as follows: $400 to interest and $618 to the principal. After the first payment, your new loan balance will be $95,382 ($96,000-$618). As the interest payments are the annual percentage of the debt amount, the second month's interest payment will reflect the 5% of $95,382. This will be $397 interest, and your principal will be $621, totaling the same monthly payment as the first month, $1,018.

SCENARIO ANALYSIS: LOWERING AN INTEREST RATE

Everyone would prefer a lower interest rate, but at what cost? If you are about to borrow $200,000 in a 30-year loan at a 5.75% interest rate, and the lender offers to lower the interest rate to 5.5% at an additional cost of $2,000, is this convenient and justifies an additional $2,000 upfront cost? Let's check.

If you choose the 5.75% rate, your monthly payment will be $1,167. If you chose the 5.5% rate, your monthly payment would be reduced by $31, and you will send the lender $1,136 per month. I calculated two savings, the accumulated monthly savings and the savings in the principal balance at each term, resulting in your total savings, at the right side of the chart. No doubt, the lower interest rate saves you money monthly and for the life of the loan. In your specific case, did it save you money if you chose the lower interest rate and paid $2,000 upfront?

	5.75%			5.50%					
30 year	Monthly Payment		Principal	Monthly Payment		Principal	Monthly	Principal	Total
	Principal	Interest	Balance	Principal	Interest	Balance	Savings	Savings	Savings
Month 1	$209	$958	$199,791	$219	$917	$199,781	$31	$10	$41
Month 12	$220	$947	$197,427	$230	$906	$197,306	$372	$121	$493
Month 24	$233	$934	$194,702	$243	$893	$194,460	$744	$242	$986
Month 36	$247	$920	$191,817	$257	$879	$191,453	$1,116	$364	**$1,480**

By the end of the 3rd year, your total savings are $1,480

4 years	$261	$906	$188,761	$272	$864	$188,277	$1,488	$484	$1,972
5 years	$277	$890	$185,524	$287	$849	$184,921	$1,860	$603	**$2,463**
10 years	$369	$798	$166,240	$377	$759	$165,082	$3,720	$1,158	**$4,878**

By the end of the 5th year, your total savings are $2,463

By the end of the 10th year, your total savings are $4,878

The savings and the expense will break even during the fifth year of the mortgage repayment, and by the end of the fifth year, you saved on paper $2,463, less the upfront cost of $2,000; you saved $463. It is up to you to decide if it is convenient for you. If you continue paying the mortgage, the savings will increase. If you decide to refinance after three years or sell the home after four years, you lose money because of purchasing the additional 0.25%.

Using an amortization schedule, you can understand the impact of a lower 0.25% interest rate. If you are charged an additional loan origination amount for reducing the interest rate by 0.25%, the amortization schedule will help determine the convenience of the interest rate reduction by evaluating the lower interest rate at the offered cost.

Interest rates vary according to the mortgage program offered and the length of the loan. There is more than one option for each term, and based on the cost associated with each interest rate, the lender will recommend the rate and its fees. In a loan advertisement, you can often see the name of a mortgage plan, the number of years, and a number representing the interest rate. There is more than one option for you to choose from, and some rates will make more financial sense than others due to the cost.

We reviewed the differences in rates and compared their long-term impact. This is accurate when you have a fixed interest rate, meaning the loan's interest rate does not change during the loan's life.

In an **Adjustable-Rate Mortgage** (ARM), the interest rate is fixed for several months or years, usually offering a lower initial interest rate compared to a fixed interest rate. After a set-in-advance number of months, which can vary from six months to ten years, the rate changes during the loan's remaining life. The new interest rate will be determined by the market condition and the loan terms as decided when the mortgage originated.

Should you be worried about a change that does not concern you and has no impact on you? Many clients shared with me their perception that ARM loans (loans with an ARM interest rate) are not a good product because they are unpredictable, and you should avoid them at all costs. They can be unpredictable after the fixed interest rate term, and still, they can be a very good product if you plan on using them just for the fixed rate term.

If you plan on staying in your house for five or six years, you will not benefit from a short-term or five-year fixed rate; however, what about a seven- or ten-year fixed rate? If you take an ARM 10, this means that for the first ten years of the loan, the lower interest rate will not change. This is a good option if you plan to sell the home before that. You have a practical, immediate gain over a hypothetical risk if you decide to stay in the house for a longer time, and interest rates will increase significantly. You can always refinance if it is more convenient at that time.

Set up a goal for the term that you will hold the property. If it is a long-term home or your forever home, the fixed interest rate is your way to go. In other scenarios, the ARM can be a good option. Let the mortgage numbers speak, and have your goals in mind to lead the way.

An interest-only mortgage is often perceived as a less-than-attractive option because you pay your monthly payments, and your debt is not reduced. Is it really a bad option?

I have a friend in New Jersey who wanted his kids to attend a specific high school. He did not want to spend money on rentals in the area, as they were costly, and he was looking to keep his monthly payments as low as possible. The housing market in that neighborhood was increasing steadily every year. Not a very high increase, but a compounding yearly benefit. He chose to buy a home and pay an interest-only mortgage. This allowed him to pay a monthly payment that was significantly less than renting, and after a few years, he sold the house with a profit. His gain was not limited to the tax-exempt capital gain when he sold the house; he also gained by lowering his monthly expense during the years he owned the house, as the monthly interest-only payment was lower than the cost of the rent.

Unfortunately, I witnessed other experiences with interest-only mortgages. A client of mine was looking to refinance. She was very optimistic as she had been paying her mortgage for a long time, and now, due to retirement, she was hoping to benefit from a refinance and lower her monthly payments. My client was unaware that she was in a **balloon mortgage** set up for 40 years, and her debt was far larger than she expected.

CHAPTER 9: SUMMARY

Mortgage Monthly Payments

can share endless examples of the times clients and friends assumed they were in a certain financial position because they were sending a high or low payment to a lender. It is deceiving to judge the cost of a product based on your monthly payment. Previously, we focused on the allocation of your monthly payments. Now, we will begin with the monthly portion of the loan payment, and continue with the impact of the payments during the life of the loan.

Your monthly mortgage payment will include your principal and interest (P&I) payments, and it can also include escrow, the payment set aside to pay monthly, annual or semiannual expenses, such as mortgage insurance, home insurance, and property taxes. According to the loan agreement, you might be able to pay only P&I and pay the property taxes and home insurance on your own when due.

 Some thoughts about escrowing:

- Some clients prefer to escrow the property taxes and home insurance, even though they are not obligated to, because they do not want to be required to pay a hefty amount annually or semi-annually. When they escrow, they avoid significant periodic expenses, and they get peace of mind knowing that they do not need to deal with this.

- If you have a fixed interest rate loan and expect the monthly payment to be fixed for the life of the loan, be aware that when the escrow increases, the monthly payment will increase accordingly. The lender has no control if the property taxes and the home insurance increase. Be on top of the home insurance payment amount. If the home insurance increases, shop around. Compare with other companies. You can replace the home insurance company. The escrow simply sets the money aside, ready to pay the required amount to the company on file.

- Are you taking advantage of any property tax benefits? Depending on your state and sometimes city, you can be eligible for property tax benefits or exemptions. Be aware to review this as needed.

Let's review more in-depth the monthly mortgage payments (principal and interest). With a **fixed interest rate**, you get one monthly amount that you must pay, which is fixed for the life of the loan until you pay off the mortgage or refinance.

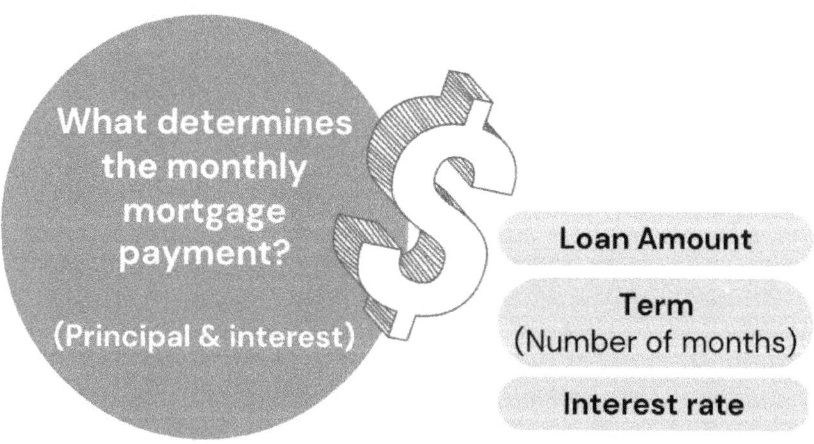

For a $200,000 30-year loan with a 5% fixed interest rate, you will pay $1,074/month.

Year	Month #	Principal Payment	Interest Payment	Total monthly Payment	Principal Balance
0	1	$241	$833	$1,074	$199,760
0	6	$245	$829	$1,074	$198,543
1	12	$252	$822	$1,074	$197,049
5	60	$307	$767	$1,074	$183,658
10	120	$394	$680	$1,074	$162,684
15	180	$506	$568	$1,074	$135,768
20	240	$649	$425	$1,074	$101,224
25	300	$833	$241	$1,074	$56,893
30	360	$1,069	$5	$1,074	$0

In the first month, just $241 will be paid towards your debt, and the rest, $833 of interest, will be delivered to the lender. Every month the amount paid to interest will be reduced, and the amount paid to principal will be increased. For example, after 12 months of payments, your interest payments will be reduced by $11; after 20 years, the monthly interest payment will be lowered to $425, adding the difference to the principal payments.

Understand the concept. The question is not how much you pay but rather who you are paying to, how your payment is divided, and how much you pay yourself. The charts on the next page show the impact in different lower and higher interest rate scenarios and compare 15 to 30 years.

ATTENTION   Why do you need to know all the details? The details will allow you to understand the concept. The general information and sales pitch, which we take into consideration when deciding what we can benefit from, has a very different impact when we use a portion of the product.

$200,000 loan, 30-year term

		Year 1		Year 20	
		1st month pay.		**12th month pay.**		**240th month pay.**	
Interest Rate	Monthly Payment	Principal	Interest	Principal	Interest	Principal	Interest
4%	**$955**	$288	$667	$299	$656	$638	$317
5%	**$1,074**	$241	$833	$251	$822	$629	$425
6%	**$1,199**	$199	$1,000	$210	$989	$656	$543

$200,000 loan, 15-year term

		Year 1		Year 10	
		1st month pay.		**12th month pay.**		**120th month pay.**	
Interest Rate	Monthly Payment	Principal	Interest	Principal	Interest	Principal	Interest
4%	**$1,479**	$812	$667	$843	$636	$1,207	$272
5%	**$1,582**	$749	$833	$783	$799	$1,227	$355
6%	**$1,688**	$687	$1,000	$727	$961	$1,245	$443

Using the numbers above, I can share with you some mortgage options that sound very appealing if you think about monthly charges and savings during the life of a loan, for example, for a $200,000 loan.

♦ Get a 30-year loan at 5%, and pay $1,074 per month, or get a 15-year loan at 4% and pay $1,479 per month. If you choose the 15-year loan, you will save $120,224 in interest!

♦ If $1,479 is too high for your monthly payment, do a 20-year loan at 4.5%, and your monthly payment will be $1,265, and compared to the 30-year option, you will save $82,840 in interest!

Many will calculate if they can afford the $1,265 or $1,479 per month, as it is wonderful to be able to save so much money. If you are certain that you will pay the mortgage in full in the expected time, you will not sell the property or refinance the mortgage before the end of the chosen term, so yes, the numbers are correct; you will save those amounts. Realistically, the average American spends

13 years in their home before selling and refinancing a few times during the life of the loan.

Generally speaking, as we saw in the charts, the charges of principal and interest are not divided into equal parts for the life of the loan, and as a result, if you decide to refinance after five years, a 15-year loan; during the five years you had the loan, you did not pay a third of the interest of what you were supposed to pay in a 15-year loan, you paid much more. Let's understand this with numbers:

A $200,000 15-year loan, 4%, during the life of the loan, you will pay $66,288 in interest. After five years of mortgage payments, your total interest paid up to this time will total $34,881.

Sometimes, I was told by clients that it was not convenient to refinance and to lower the interest rate because if the borrower sent more money monthly, the loan would be paid off faster, thus avoiding the refinance costs. However, if you had a high-interest loan and you sent more money every month, you would still be paying the high interest, and less money would go toward the principal. Therefore, it is advantageous in most cases to have a lower-interest loan, pending the additional costs.

We will continue and review the impact of your monthly payment on your principal balance, the amount you owe, and how much your home really costs you.

What is the market interest rate? You might not perceive a difference in a matter of weeks, but there might be a significant difference in a matter of months. Is the interest rate lower? Do you have equity in the home to consolidate debt if needed? If so, you can address this in addition to benefitting from a lower interest rate. There are many options; sometimes, you must wait and improve your current qualification in order to get where you want to be.

$200,000 loan, 30-year term

Interest Rate	Total interest paid for the life of the loan	Principal Balance			
		after 1 year	after 2 years	after 5 years	after 10 years
4%	$143,739	$196,478	$192,812	$180,895	$157,568
5%	$186,512	$197,049	$193,948	$183,657	$162,684
6%	$231,676	$197,544	$194,937	$186,109	$167,371

$200,000 loan, 15-year term

Interest Rate	Total interest paid for the life of the loan	Principal Balance			
		after 1 year	after 2 years	after 5 years	after 10 years
4%	$66,288	$190,067	$179,729	$146,118	$80,329
5%	$84,686	$190,812	$181,155	$149,114	$83,809
6%	$103,788	$191,517	$182,510	$152,018	$87,298

To conclude the mortgage monthly payment options, I want you to be aware of the option of recast.

ATTENTION A mortgage **recast** is when a lender recalculates the monthly payments on your current loan based on the outstanding principal balance and the remaining term. It is applicable if you make extra loan payments during the life of the loan, and it does not matter if you made the extra payments regularly or as a one-time large amount. Some lenders will require you to qualify if you paid a specific amount over the last 12 months. A result of a recast will be a lower monthly payment, compared to the original amount required, before adding the extra payments you made.

As it is not considered a refinance, you do not need to apply with an updated income, credit score, or other criteria. It is simply a recast.

SCENARIO ANALYSIS—RECAST

Suppose you took a $350,000 mortgage ten years ago: a 30-years term at a 5%. Your monthly payment is $1,879. Every month you paid $2,500, and six months ago, you sent an additional one-time payment of $8,000.

Your current balance is $180,267. Under the same mortgage, without refinancing, you will pay the mortgage much sooner than the 20 years remaining on paper if you had not sent the additional payments. Due to some unforeseen situation, you prefer now to reduce the monthly payment as much as possible, even less than the original $1,879.

If you comply with the recast requirements of your lender, the lender will recalculate the remaining balance of $180,267 over the remaining number of years, in this case, 20 years, with the same interest rate in your current mortgage, and the new monthly payment will be $1,190.

CHAPTER 10: SUMMARY

MORTGAGE MONTHLY PAYMENTS

Monthly payments
With a fixed interest rate, the total P&I payments remain the same. The principal and interest amount change monthly.

Payments during the life of a fully amortized loan
In the first years of a loan, the majority of the monthly payment pays off the interest. The amount allocated to pay the principal increases monthly.

Recast
If you made additional payments to the loan, subject to the lender's terms, the lender can recalculte the payment for the remaining principal, with the current remaining term and existing interest rate.

Qualifications for a Mortgage

You can approach a lender and accept your approval terms or denial as a fact, or you can prepare in advance and get the best terms for your new mortgage. Sometimes, if the market rates are good, or you have the urgency to refinance or get a mortgage in a certain time frame, it is not relevant to wait, but you will want to ensure you can qualify. Three core aspects of mortgage qualification you need to be on top:

- Income
- Credit score and credit report
- Debt-to-Income ratio

Income

The lender would like to ensure, as much as possible, that you have a reliable source of income to pay back the debt. You can be employed or self-employed. Each program will have different requirements for work history, the length of time you are working in this line of work, and what gaps in the work timeline can impact your eligibility. A lender may ask for tax returns, W-2s, and pay stubs for your employed work income. When you are self-employed, you may be asked to provide a profit and loss report and bank account statements in addition to the income taxes.

If you present passive income, such as social security or a pension, you need to provide the documentation, and it can vary among lenders: a verification letter from Social Security, the Veteran Affairs, or your pension. Sometimes, you can provide proof of income by presenting the deposits to your bank account.

Credit Score and Credit Report

Credit inquiries are an integral part of applying for a mortgage; you can't avoid that. When a lender runs your credit check, they gather valuable information to predict your strength as a borrower. You can prepare in advance by being aware of your credit strength.

Credit bureaus are companies that collect information about individuals' credit and calculate their credit scores accordingly. Equifax, Experian, and Transunion are the three major credit bureaus in the U.S. The credit bureaus provide credit reports, a record of the borrower's credit history from several sources. Based on the credit report information, an algorithm calculates the credit score; it predicts your credit behavior, such as how likely you are to pay a loan back on time, based on information from your credit reports. The FICO credit score ranges from 300 to 850.

A good credit score can benefit you in two ways: You need a minimum credit score to qualify for a mortgage, and the higher the credit score, the better the terms.

Many mortgages require a minimum credit score of 620. Some government-backed mortgages have lower credit requirements.

- Check your credit score. You need to know your current credit score and if it is necessary to improve it.
- Request from the credit bureaus a copy of your credit reports, review them and look for anything requiring attention.

Sometimes some errors need to be addressed. When you check your credit, there is no negative impact on your credit score. A few times, when I reviewed the credit report with my clients, they were surprised to find items they were unaware of or other mistakes that needed to be addressed. A few times, there were collections on medical bills that the client was unaware of, as they had been sent to an old address. Other times, their credit report was not updated to mark a debt as paid off. All this can be addressed, but you must be aware of it first.

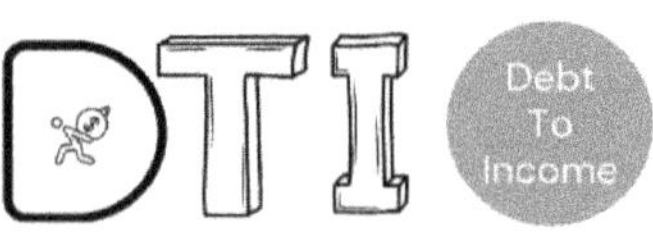

Debt-to-Income

The Debt-to-Income (DTI) ratio is used to assess the level of risk associated with lending money to a prospective borrower, as it reflects how much of the borrower's income is allocated to pay off debts. It is a percentage amount. There can be a big difference between what you need to qualify for a mortgage, what is possibly reflecting your living expenses, and what should be the limit you define. First, let us understand how the income and the debts are calculated, proceeding with what should be the DTI convenient for you.

The income is calculated according to the gross income based on the documentation you provide the MLO. The income can be from your employment, business, passive income, Social Security, and more. All income will need to be verified. If the income is not enough, and someone co-signs your mortgage, the co-signers income will be considered, as well as their debt.

Your credit report will provide detailed information on your monthly obligations, the minimum payments for credit cards, car payments, student loans, etc. In addition, your home expenses will be calculated, including the mortgage, taxes, home insurance, and even HOA. When you divide the total monthly minimum expenses by your gross monthly income, you receive a percentage, your Debt-to-Income.

What do mortgage programs require as maximum DTI?

Conventional loans can be under 50%, some lenders will lower the limit to 36%, and others will require under 45%. From those total percentages, the debt is divided into front-end and back-end.

Front-end DTI reflects how much of your gross income goes towards housing costs. (P&I, taxes, insurance, HOA).

Back-end DTI reflects all your required minimum monthly debt.

There are different approaches and suggestions as to how much should your maximum DTI be.

Be aware of all that is required, as you need to comply under those limitations in order to qualify for a mortgage. Now, put this aside and do your own math.

Assume a lender will qualify you with 57% DTI, in an FHA loan. Should you really do this? The 57% reflects the gross amount. It is not a percentage of the money you bring home. You have other expenses on food, gasoline, clothes, health, and more that are not included in the DTI. How much money really is left, and do you feel comfortable with the result, even though you can qualify? Do your own math on top of the lender.

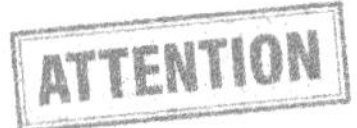

Another aspect to consider is who needs to be on the mortgage and who you want to be on the mortgage. It is not the same thing.

Let's assume a couple owns a home, and both of their names are on the title. Both are on the mortgage. The mortgage payments are wired from the couple's joint checking account. What does it mean?

From a debt perspective, each one is responsible for the mortgage payment. On each individual credit report, their mortgage will be noted for the life of the loan. It is not related to the income of each owner.

It can be decided that both are on the title, and as owner #2 does not have a good credit score, just owner #1 will be on the mortgage as long as the DTI of owner #1 complies with the requirements. If the DTI is too high, it will be necessary to add owner #2 to show additional income, and it will be possible only after owner #2 improves his credit.

CHAPTER 11: SUMMARY

MORTGAGE QUALIFICATION

Qualified Income
Employed, self-employed, or passive income. Minimum length of time. Required documentation.

Credit
Some mortgages require a minimum of a 620 credit score. Government loans will allow a lower score. The credit reports will provide information on bankruptcies, disputes, and other debt.

Debt-to-Income
A percentage reflecting your total monthly minimum debt payment, divided by your gross monthly qualified income.

Mortgage Process

There are two scenarios where you would approach an MLO inquiring about a mortgage; when you plan to purchase a home and pay for it with a mortgage and when you are looking to refinance your current mortgage.

When you are looking to buy a home, you will ask the MLO for a pre-approval letter. This means you review your finances with your lender, and based on the information provided, the lender will give you a letter with the loan amount you can qualify for. You will use this letter when you present an offer to buy a home, as most sellers would like to know that the buyer is qualified to obtain a loan to purchase the home. You are ready to begin the mortgage application process when your offer is accepted. At this point, the following process is very similar to when you want to refinance the mortgage of your current home.

There can be a gap of days, weeks, or two months from when you obtained your preapproval letter until you find your home and are under contract, ready to proceed. Along the same vein, there can be a significant time gap between when you initially inquired about refinancing your mortgage and when you are ready and willing to proceed.

Shopping for a mortgage

I encourage you to approach multiple lenders and shop around. The mortgage industry is a heavily regulated market; still, you will find differences between one lender and others. Not all lenders provide all the loan options. In addition, some will provide different rates and costs, some will service the loan after **closing**, and some will not.

I would like you to know what to expect when shopping for a mortgage, what information you need to provide, and what information needs to be provided to you. Understand the terms used to compare lenders' information accurately. Only after knowing your options should you decide which lender you would like to work with, and then you will fill out the mortgage application, following with the loan process up to the closing.

Information you will provide to the lender

When contacting a lender, you will need to provide personal information so the lender can check your initial eligibility for a mortgage and provide details on the proposed options. General requests, such as asking the MLO to provide information on what is the best rate today, are irrelevant, as any number can be thrown in the air. You would benefit from accurate information. You cannot and should not decide your path based on possible theoretical options, wishful thinking, or irrelevant promises. You want to know the program you should choose, the interest rates, and the costs. Let's review what information is needed from you and, as a result, what information you can expect to receive and what information you should compare between lenders.

Some of the information you will provide will include your name, marital status, date of birth, Social Security number, and information on your income, job, and home. The same is true for any other person listed on the mortgage. Other information might include VA eligibility, current assets, and more.

The personal information will be required to run a credit check. The credit report can provide the actual credit score and other information, such as the exact total and monthly debt amounts, any information on other properties that are not free and clear, past bankruptcies, amount of debt in dispute, number of late mortgage payments (over 30 days), etc. All of the above will impact your eligibility and possible loan terms.

When a lender runs your credit for mortgage purposes, you have a window of forty-five days in which your credit can be checked multiple times by other lenders (only if you provide your consent to do so), and it won't count as an additional hard inquiry. Remember, this rule applies only for inquiries for mortgage purposes. For this reason, do not be concerned if each mortgage lender asks to run your credit. It is a hard inquiry that has a negative impact on your credit score, and it is a necessary part of applying for a mortgage to receive accurate information from lenders.

The lender will need to know if you are requesting a mortgage for a primary residence, a second home, or an investment. You will be asked about your employment and your income, for income eligibility purposes and DTI calculations.

At this point, details are important, as they can change your options. You do not want to skip an opportunity because you just want a quick number and move on to the next lender's proposal.

Let me share an example of what opportunities can arise from getting into details. A client called me because a year earlier, she bought a house for the son and daughter-in-law to live in. When she bought the house, she got the loan terms of an investment property, as she did not intend to live in the home. The interest rate was high, and this home was expected to be the forever home for her son and daughter-in-law. Our goal was to reduce the interest rate significantly, saving on interest payments for the life of the loan without increasing the monthly payment, and it was her preference to shorten the twenty-nine years left on the mortgage. As the son and daughter-in-law lived in the house, I suggested adding them to the refinanced mortgage. The son's credit score would not have made it possible for him to apply for a mortgage, and the daughter-in-law had a good credit score but no income. The solution was to have the parents and daughter-in-law on the mortgage; the three had a good credit score, and the income was calculated based on the parent's income. As it was the primary residence of one of the mortgage's principals, they got an excellent rate for a 20-year mortgage, reducing the monthly payment and cutting off years from the life of the mortgage.

Information the lender will provide you

What information should you expect from the lender? A lender should provide you with a suggested mortgage and its terms. Before understanding a loan's terms, you need to know the following:

- Whatever the lender offers, if you do not lock the interest rate, it is not guaranteed this offer will be relevant tomorrow. The interest rates change daily and are different from one program to another. When you choose a program and decide to proceed with the application, the lender will lock the interest rate.
- You can compare different programs or the same program with different terms: for example, 20 years vs. 30 years.
- Every program has more than one interest rate option, and usually, there is one rate that makes more sense than the others, comparing the rate and its cost. For example, a 30-year conventional loan can have options of 4.5%, 4.75%, 4.875%, and 5%, and each interest rate will require a different points cost, which means a different origination cost.
- Based on your goals, you might benefit from a lower or higher interest rate. How can a higher interest rate make

sense? Let me share with you a story about a client. She was interested in refinancing to put herself in a better position because, in one year, she was planning to sell her home and move to another state. For her, the best option was a loan with no origination costs, and in her case, she chose a higher interest rate. She consolidated all of her debts and cashed out the needed amount to buy a car with no additional loan. Because of the interest rate and a lender's credit, she ended up with $0 closing costs, and when we compared how much she would pay monthly with the high-interest option during a year and a year and a half option vs. if she would have gotten the lower interest rate but paid the closing costs, she ended up saving a significant amount of money. Her total monthly expenses were reduced, and her credit score will improve significantly as all her debts are now paid off. As she lowered her monthly expenses, she plans to save for the down payment on her next home.

Understanding a loan's various terms

When a lender pulls your credit report, he is obligated to provide you a **loan estimate** (LE) up to three days after pulling your credit, regardless of if you decide to proceed with a loan application or not.

The best way to compare different lenders' proposals is to compare the loan estimates, as they use the same format. You want to make sure you compare apples to apples between programs and lenders.

I remember speaking with a client about a refinance option, and he explained that he received loan estimates from several lenders, and one lender said he could offer him more cash back. I asked to see the loan estimate, and we compared each item. The other lender estimated a lower mortgage payoff amount, which resulted theoretically, on paper, in more cash back. This illusion of more money back to the client was deceiving, as the actual mortgage final payoff amount should be the same regardless of which lender you use to refinance. When you review the initial loan estimate, the lender might not be able to provide the exact final payoff amount of the existing loan. Be aware of the discrepancies. In the case of the client mentioned, the charges for the cost of the loan offered by the other lender were higher, which would have resulted in less cash back to the client.

To avoid misleading or confusing information, we will review a sample of a mortgage loan estimate, a three-page form.

Let's walk thru the three pages of the loan estimate and understand the information provided.

General terms

In the loan estimate sample, you will be able to review the information for a conventional 30-year fixed-rate mortgage. The property to be purchased costs $180,000, the borrower will put 10% down ($18,000), and the mortgage for the amount of $162,000 will cover the remaining 90% of the cost. Up to now, it sounds like general information that I can ask any lender, expecting to receive the information on what the lender has to offer in return. For that purpose, we review and understand what information we can find in the loan estimate, and—the most important part—understand where we can expect the differences between the offers of the lenders.

If different lenders offer a loan with the same loan amount, term, and interest rate, the P&I will be exactly the same. The differences will be in the cost of the loan (charges for origination and services provided), the eligibility criteria acceptable by the lender, and whether the lender will service the loan or not.

The first page of the LE will detail general information about your agreed-upon terms and estimated monthly costs.

FICUS BANK

4321 Random Boulevard • Somecity, ST 12340

Save this Loan Estimate to compare with your Closing Disclosure.

Loan Estimate

DATE ISSUED	2/15/2013	**LOAN TERM**	30 years
APPLICANTS	Michael Jones and Mary Stone	**PURPOSE**	Purchase
	123 Anywhere Street	**PRODUCT**	Fixed Rate
	Anytown, ST 12345	**LOAN TYPE**	☒ Conventional ☐FHA ☐VA ☐ _______
PROPERTY	456 Somewhere Avenue	**LOAN ID #**	123456789
	Anytown, ST 12345	**RATE LOCK**	☐NO ☒ YES, until 4/16/2013 at 5:00 p.m. EDT
SALE PRICE	$180,000		

*Before closing, your interest rate, points, and lender credits can change unless you lock the interest rate. All other estimated closing costs expire on **3/4/2013** at 5:00 p.m. EDT*

Loan Terms

		Can this amount increase after closing?
Loan Amount	$162,000	**NO**
Interest Rate	3.875%	**NO**
Monthly Principal & Interest *See Projected Payments below for your Estimated Total Monthly Payment*	$761.78	**NO**
		Does the loan have these features?
Prepayment Penalty		**YES** • As high as **$3,240** if you pay off the loan during the first 2 years
Balloon Payment		**NO**

Projected Payments

Payment Calculation	Years 1-7	Years 8-30
Principal & Interest	$761.78	$761.78
Mortgage Insurance	+ 82	+ —
Estimated Escrow *Amount can increase over time*	+ 206	+ 206
Estimated Total Monthly Payment	$1,050	$968

Estimated Taxes, Insurance & Assessments *Amount can increase over time*	$206 a month	**This estimate includes** ☒ Property Taxes ☒ Homeowner's Insurance ☐ Other: *See Section G on page 2 for escrowed property costs. You must pay for other property costs separately.*	**In escrow?** YES YES

Costs at Closing

Estimated Closing Costs	$8,054	Includes $5,672 in Loan Costs + $2,382 in Other Costs – $0 in Lender Credits. *See page 2 for details.*
Estimated Cash to Close	$16,054	Includes Closing Costs. *See Calculating Cash to Close on page 2 for details.*

Closing Cost Details

Loan Costs

A. Origination Charges	$1,802
.25 % of Loan Amount (Points)	$405
Application Fee	$300
Underwriting Fee	$1,097

B. Services You Cannot Shop For	$672
Appraisal Fee	$405
Credit Report Fee	$30
Flood Determination Fee	$20
Flood Monitoring Fee	$32
Tax Monitoring Fee	$75
Tax Status Research Fee	$110

C. Services You Can Shop For	$3,198
Pest Inspection Fee	$135
Survey Fee	$65
Title – Insurance Binder	$700
Title – Lender's Title Policy	$535
Title – Settlement Agent Fee	$502
Title – Title Search	$1,261

D. TOTAL LOAN COSTS (A + B + C)	$5,672

Other Costs

E. Taxes and Other Government Fees	$85
Recording Fees and Other Taxes	$85
Transfer Taxes	

F. Prepaids	$867
Homeowner's Insurance Premium (6 months)	$605
Mortgage Insurance Premium (months)	
Prepaid Interest ($17.44 per day for 15 days @ 3.875%)	$262
Property Taxes (months)	

G. Initial Escrow Payment at Closing		$413
Homeowner's Insurance	$100.83 per month for 2 mo.	$202
Mortgage Insurance	per month for mo.	
Property Taxes	$105.30 per month for 2 mo.	$211

H. Other	$1,017
Title – Owner's Title Policy (optional)	$1,017

I. TOTAL OTHER COSTS (E + F + G + H)	$2,382

J. TOTAL CLOSING COSTS	$8,054
D + I	$8,054
Lender Credits	

Calculating Cash to Close

Total Closing Costs (J)	$8,054
Closing Costs Financed (Paid from your Loan Amount)	$0
Down Payment/Funds from Borrower	$18,000
Deposit	– $10,000
Funds for Borrower	$0
Seller Credits	$0
Adjustments and Other Credits	$0
Estimated Cash to Close	$16,054

Additional Information About This Loan

LENDER	Ficus Bank
NMLS/__ LICENSE ID	
LOAN OFFICER	Joe Smith
NMLS/__ LICENSE ID	12345
EMAIL	joesmith@ficusbank.com
PHONE	123-456-7890

MORTGAGE BROKER	
NMLS/__ LICENSE ID	
LOAN OFFICER	
NMLS/__ LICENSE ID	
EMAIL	
PHONE	

Comparisons — Use these measures to compare this loan with other loans.

In 5 Years	$56,582	Total you will have paid in principal, interest, mortgage insurance, and loan costs.
	$15,773	Principal you will have paid off.
Annual Percentage Rate (APR)	4.274%	Your costs over the loan term expressed as a rate. This is not your interest rate.
Total Interest Percentage (TIP)	69.45%	The total amount of interest that you will pay over the loan term as a percentage of your loan amount.

Other Considerations

Appraisal	We may order an appraisal to determine the property's value and charge you for this appraisal. We will promptly give you a copy of any appraisal, even if your loan does not close. You can pay for an additional appraisal for your own use at your own cost.
Assumption	If you sell or transfer this property to another person, we ☐ will allow, under certain conditions, this person to assume this loan on the original terms. ☒ will not allow assumption of this loan on the original terms.
Homeowner's Insurance	This loan requires homeowner's insurance on the property, which you may obtain from a company of your choice that we find acceptable.
Late Payment	If your payment is more than 15 days late, we will charge a late fee of 5% *of the monthly principal and interest payment.*
Refinance	Refinancing this loan will depend on your future financial situation, the property value, and market conditions. You may not be able to refinance this loan.
Servicing	We intend ☐ to service your loan. If so, you will make your payments to us. ☒ to transfer servicing of your loan.

Confirm Receipt

By signing, you are only confirming that you have received this form. You do not have to accept this loan because you have signed or received this form.

_______________________________   _______________
Applicant Signature   Date   Co-Applicant Signature   Date

The upper part will describe the type of loan, the loan terms, and the information on the principals of this transaction. In the chart below the general information, you will read the loan terms: the loan amount, the interest rate, and the monthly payment amount for principal and interest. It will mark with yes or no if the loan amount, the interest rate, or the mortgage repayment amount can change after closing. In the example provided, the amounts will not change because it is a conventional loan with a fixed interest rate.

A prepayment penalty means that if you decide to pay off the mortgage earlier than initially planned, there can be a penalty. This information will detail if it applies to your mortgage or not.

A balloon payment occurs when the mortgage is not fully amortized over the term of the loan, and there is a balance due when the final repayment of the loan is due.

Projected payments

The projected payments include the principal and interest previously calculated and the other expenses such as property taxes, homeowners' insurance, homeowners' association if relevant, and mortgage insurance. Let's review the chart in the sample of the Loan Estimate:

- The principal and interest monthly payment does not change for the life of the loan.
- The mortgage insurance (marked $82) in a conventional loan is charged because the down payment is less than 20% of the purchase price. The mortgage insurance can be charged over the entire life of the loan (as in an FHA loan); in this case, it indicates that it will be charged for the first seven years.
- The estimated escrow details includes the property tax and homeowners' insurance, and it does not include the homeowners association dues.

At the bottom of the page, the total closing costs and cash to close can be confusing, and it is better to review those totals on the following page, so you can understand what each amount includes.

The second page will explain all the costs that will impact the cash needed to close: The charges will be divided into loan costs and other costs.

Loan costs

On the second page of the LE, you will review in detail the charges for the origination of the loan and the services provided. In addition, under tab J, there is an option for a lender's discount by giving you a lender's credit. You should compare those costs and credits.

Other costs

Under the tab "other costs," you will review any escrow and prepaid charges. The lender will calculate these based on the actual expected costs and the due dates.

The total closing costs will vary significantly if you escrow or not. Sometimes the total closing costs seem high, and some borrowers can be upset that the lender charges them high amounts. Still, when you analyze it, you need to realize that you cannot consider the payment for your homeowner's insurance or your property taxes as a payment that your lender benefits from, even though it is titled "total closing costs."

The loan amount and cash to close

Looking just at the loan amount, or cash to close, is inaccurate. When updating the payoff amount in a refinance or an updated escrow, the required loan amount can change and impact the required cash you need to bring to the table. This is why you should never overlook the actual costs of the loan.

Escrow account

The escrow on an existing mortgage is your money. When you refinance a mortgage and are currently escrowing on the active mortgage, you will be reimbursed the amount left in the escrow account of the current mortgage, and the new mortgage will calculate a new escrow. There are a few ways to be reimbursed on the current escrow. Your lender can send you a check after closing, your escrow's credit can be deducted from your payoff amount, or if you refinance with the same current lender, some lenders will allow the escrow on your current mortgage to roll into the new escrow account.

Check with your lender how the escrow will be reimbursed to you, and be sure to review this when you check the payoff amount. This option is relevant if you are refinancing. If you are purchasing a property, there is no existing escrow account to reimburse.

Other aspects of the escrow to understand in the loan estimate are the prepaid amounts to escrow. Let's understand how it works. When you escrow, you make monthly payments to cover the yearly or semiannual expenses such as home insurance and property taxes.

Theoretically, if property taxes and home insurance total $2,400 annually, you will require a monthly payment of $200, resulting in enough money to cover the annual cost. There are two things to be aware of:

- As property taxes and home insurance increase, the escrow will increase. Often, the information about the rise and the updated amount will not be known twelve months in advance, resulting in a deficit in the escrow, and you will need to catch up with that different amount. For example, with the previous scenario where the monthly escrow was $200 per month, let's assume that property taxes need to be paid in three months, and you get an updated bill with an increase of $120 annually. This would reflect $10 per month, but as the payment needs to be paid in three months, you will have just an additional $30 in the escrow account, and you will need to make up for the $90 difference. Moving forward, as you will have twelve payments to pay the next bill, if it is not increased further, paying the additional $10 per month will be enough for the $120 increase. The timing is the key in this case, as in the prepaid amounts.

♦ With the new escrow account, you must prepay in closing the balance needed to pay property taxes or the home insurance on time and in full. Let's assume you need to pay $1,200 for home insurance in four months and in seven months, the taxes of $1200 will be due. The lender calculates the monthly escrow payments from the first payment of the new mortgage, and any difference and reserves needed for the total amount are calculated in the prepaid escrow at the closing costs.

The monthly escrow amount and the prepaid escrow amount are not flexible unless you change a home insurance provider to one with a lower premium or you are eligible for a property tax discount that was not applied.

This means you should not assume that one lender is charging you a lower loan cost because the escrow required is less than the other lender. Probably one of the lender's escrow amounts is inaccurate, and it will need to be updated before closing. When you compare programs, compare what is relevant.

Another impact of the different programs' fees that should be reflected in the loan cost is the VA funding fee when you do a VA loan and the prepaid mortgage insurance premium when you do a FHA loan.

Choose a program and a loan

You choose a program and receive the updated loan estimate with all the information in writing. When the MLO locks in the mortgage's interest rate, your interest rate will not change as long as you close in a specific time frame.

Gather documentation and sign the application

You will provide your income documents and others, as your lender requires. When you sign the application, you begin the process.

Legally, you can cancel any time until the closing of the home purchase or up to three days after closing when you refinance. For example, if you refinance and expect to receive cash back, the disbursement will occur three days after closing completion simply because you have the right to cancel the transaction during those three days.

After signing the loan application, your mortgage is processed. You need constant contact with your lender as documentation, signatures, or other clarifications might be required.

Home appraisal

The lender will order an appraisal. The lender wants to appraise the home's value and ensure he/she is working with the correct LTV. The home appraisal can match the price you thought about when speaking with the lender, and it can be higher or lower.

How do the appraisal results impact your plans? Let's review the different scenarios.

If an appraisal comes in higher or lower, it will have a different impact if you are purchasing a new home, or refinancing an existing one.

♦   When an appraisal comes in higher:

If you buy a house, and the appraised value is higher than the price you agreed upon, great. You are under contract; you should close on the price agreed upon.

If you are refinancing and the appraised value is higher than the originally estimated when planning the refinance, your LTV will be lower than the initially calculated, and there is no downside to this. If you plan on **cashing out** on your equity, you might be able to cash out more money if relevant to you.

♦   When the appraisal comes in lower:

If you buy a house, and the appraisal comes in lower than the purchase price on the contract, the lender will limit the loan amount based on the loan percentage of the new home's appraised value.

Let's understand this with an example. You are under contract for a $300,000 home, and you plan on putting 20% down ($60,000) and borrowing the remaining 80% ($240,000). The appraisal came back at $280,000, and as the bank would finance 80% of the home value, the loan would be reduced to 80% of the new appraised value, from $240,000 to $224,000.

There are two aspects to consider: the home value and the cash you need to bring to closing. Do you feel comfortable paying over the home's value? Sometimes, this is a reality because it is a seller's market or a specific home is highly desired due to a location or a renovation. If you are not comfortable overpaying, pending if you have an **appraisal rider** to the purchase contract, you can decide to re-negotiate the terms with the owner or terminate the agreement. You also need to reevaluate the impact of the additional cash required. Are you capable of paying the additional cash at closing, or do you need to change the loan's terms by increasing the LTV, and limiting the required cash to the original amount calculated? In the example discussed, if you want to limit the down payment to

$60,000, the $240,000 loan will reflect just under 86% LTV. Review your options with your MLO.

If you are refinancing and the appraisal came in lower, you need to see if there is any impact on the future mortgage, and if there is, what is the financial impact on the monthly payments or ability to achieve your goals, such as a cash-out transaction.

SCENARIO ANALYSIS: LOWER APPRAISAL

Case #1, purchase: You plan to buy a $300,000 property with an FHA loan, and a 3.5% down payment.

The appraisal came back at $280,000 instead of $300,000.

You initially calculated 3.5% down, $10,500 for a down payment, and borrowing the other 96.5%. Now, with the lower appraisal, the total loan amount cannot exceed $270,200 (96.5% of $280,000). You can proceed with the loan if you come up with the difference in addition to the down payment that you calculated initially, totaling $29,800.

Case #2, refinance: Five years ago, you bought a house at $250,000 with 5% down. The loan balance, which was originally at $237,500, is now $218,090. You pay mortgage insurance, and as you believe the home value has increased, you want to refinance, reduce the interest rate, and cash out to pay off some credit cards. You think the home is valued at $320,000, and the maximum allowed in cash out is 80% from LTV, so you plan the new loan amount to be $256,000; dropping off the mortgage insurance and paying off credit cards at considerable savings.

With the new appraisal at $280,000, the maximum loan amount was reduced to $224,000, and with the cost to refinance, you will not have much cash back. You may decide to proceed and refinance if the other terms make sense, such as if you will achieve a significantly reduced interest rate. You do not need to refinance just to drop off the mortgage insurance from a conventional loan, as after a specific period of time from the home purchase or after a significant renovation, you can ask your current lender to send an appraiser. You will be charged for this, and if the mortgage balance is under 80% of the updated home value, you will not pay the mortgage insurance any longer.

Underwriting and final review

In this process, the lender reviews all the documentation and related information, verify employment, income, assets, debt, title, and other property-related details, so you can be clear to close. You will get a loan **closing statement** with the final details about the loan.

Closing Disclosure

This form is a statement of final loan terms and closing costs. Compare this document with your Loan Estimate.

Closing Information

Date Issued	4/15/2013
Closing Date	4/15/2013
Disbursement Date	4/15/2013
Settlement Agent	Epsilon Title Co.
File #	12-3456
Property	456 Somewhere Ave
	Anytown, ST 12345
Sale Price	$180,000

Transaction Information

Borrower	Michael Jones and Mary Stone
	123 Anywhere Street
	Anytown, ST 12345
Seller	Steve Cole and Amy Doe
	321 Somewhere Drive
	Anytown, ST 12345
Lender	Ficus Bank

Loan Information

Loan Term	30 years
Purpose	Purchase
Product	Fixed Rate
Loan Type	☒ Conventional ☐ FHA ☐ VA ☐ ___
Loan ID #	123456789
MIC #	000654321

Loan Terms

		Can this amount increase after closing?
Loan Amount	$162,000	**NO**
Interest Rate	3.875%	**NO**
Monthly Principal & Interest *See Projected Payments below for your Estimated Total Monthly Payment*	$761.78	**NO**
		Does the loan have these features?
Prepayment Penalty		**YES** • **As high as $3,240** if you pay off the loan during the first 2 years
Balloon Payment		**NO**

Projected Payments

Payment Calculation	Years 1-7	Years 8-30
Principal & Interest	$761.78	$761.78
Mortgage Insurance	+ 82.35	+ —
Estimated Escrow *Amount can increase over time*	+ 206.13	+ 206.13
Estimated Total Monthly Payment	**$1,050.26**	**$967.91**

Estimated Taxes, Insurance & Assessments *Amount can increase over time* *See page 4 for details*	**$356.13** a month	**This estimate includes** ☒ Property Taxes ☒ Homeowner's Insurance ☒ Other: Homeowner's Association Dues *See Escrow Account on page 4 for details. You must pay for other property costs separately.*	**In escrow?** YES YES NO

Costs at Closing

Closing Costs	$9,712.10	Includes $4,694.05 in Loan Costs + $5,018.05 in Other Costs – $0 in Lender Credits. *See page 2 for details.*
Cash to Close	$14,147.26	Includes Closing Costs. *See Calculating Cash to Close on page 3 for details.*

Closing Cost Details

Loan Costs	Borrower-Paid At Closing	Borrower-Paid Before Closing	Seller-Paid At Closing	Seller-Paid Before Closing	Paid by Others
A. Origination Charges	**$1,802.00**				
01 0.25 % of Loan Amount (Points)	$405.00				
02 Application Fee	$300.00				
03 Underwriting Fee	$1,097.00				
04					
05					
06					
07					
08					
B. Services Borrower Did Not Shop For	**$236.55**				
01 Appraisal Fee to John Smith Appraisers Inc.					$405.00
02 Credit Report Fee to Information Inc.		$29.80			
03 Flood Determination Fee to Info Co.	$20.00				
04 Flood Monitoring Fee to Info Co.	$31.75				
05 Tax Monitoring Fee to Info Co.	$75.00				
06 Tax Status Research Fee to Info Co.	$80.00				
07					
08					
09					
10					
C. Services Borrower Did Shop For	**$2,655.50**				
01 Pest Inspection Fee to Pests Co.	$120.50				
02 Survey Fee to Surveys Co.	$85.00				
03 Title – Insurance Binder to Epsilon Title Co.	$650.00				
04 Title – Lender's Title Insurance to Epsilon Title Co.	$500.00				
05 Title – Settlement Agent Fee to Epsilon Title Co.	$500.00				
06 Title – Title Search to Epsilon Title Co.	$800.00				
07					
08					
D. TOTAL LOAN COSTS (Borrower-Paid)	**$4,694.05**				
Loan Costs Subtotals (A + B + C)	$4,664.25	$29.80			

Other Costs	Borrower-Paid At Closing	Borrower-Paid Before Closing	Seller-Paid At Closing	Seller-Paid Before Closing	Paid by Others
E. Taxes and Other Government Fees	**$85.00**				
01 Recording Fees Deed: $40.00 Mortgage: $45.00	$85.00				
02 Transfer Tax to Any State			$950.00		
F. Prepaids	**$2,120.80**				
01 Homeowner's Insurance Premium (12 mo.) to Insurance Co.	$1,209.96				
02 Mortgage Insurance Premium (mo.)					
03 Prepaid Interest ($17.44 per day from 4/15/13 to 5/1/13)	$279.04				
04 Property Taxes (6 mo.) to Any County USA	$631.80				
05					
G. Initial Escrow Payment at Closing	**$412.25**				
01 Homeowner's Insurance $100.83 per month for 2 mo.	$201.66				
02 Mortgage Insurance per month for mo.					
03 Property Taxes $105.30 per month for 2 mo.	$210.60				
04					
05					
06					
07					
08 Aggregate Adjustment	– 0.01				
H. Other	**$2,400.00**				
01 HOA Capital Contribution to HOA Acre Inc.	$500.00				
02 HOA Processing Fee to HOA Acre Inc.	$150.00				
03 Home Inspection Fee to Engineers Inc.	$750.00			$750.00	
04 Home Warranty Fee to XYZ Warranty Inc.			$450.00		
05 Real Estate Commission to Alpha Real Estate Broker			$5,700.00		
06 Real Estate Commission to Omega Real Estate Broker			$5,700.00		
07 Title – Owner's Title Insurance (optional) to Epsilon Title Co.	$1,000.00				
08					
I. TOTAL OTHER COSTS (Borrower-Paid)	**$5,018.05**				
Other Costs Subtotals (E + F + G + H)	$5,018.05				

J. TOTAL CLOSING COSTS (Borrower-Paid)	Borrower-Paid At Closing	Borrower-Paid Before Closing	Seller-Paid At Closing	Seller-Paid Before Closing	Paid by Others
J. TOTAL CLOSING COSTS (Borrower-Paid)	**$9,712.10**				
Closing Costs Subtotals (D + I)	$9,682.30	$29.80	$12,800.00	$750.00	$405.00
Lender Credits					

Calculating Cash to Close

Use this table to see what has changed from your Loan Estimate.

	Loan Estimate	Final	Did this change?
Total Closing Costs (J)	$8,054.00	$9,712.10	**YES** · See **Total Loan Costs (D)** and **Total Other Costs (I)**
Closing Costs Paid Before Closing	$0	- $29.80	**YES** · You paid these Closing Costs **before closing**
Closing Costs Financed (Paid from your Loan Amount)	$0	$0	**NO**
Down Payment/Funds from Borrower	$18,000.00	$18,000.00	**NO**
Deposit	- $10,000.00	- $10,000.00	**NO**
Funds for Borrower	$0	$0	**NO**
Seller Credits	$0	- $2,500.00	**YES** · See Seller Credits in **Section L**
Adjustments and Other Credits	$0	- $1,035.04	**YES** · See details in **Sections K and L**
Cash to Close	$16,054.00	$14,147.26	

Summaries of Transactions

Use this table to see a summary of your transaction.

BORROWER'S TRANSACTION

K. Due from Borrower at Closing	$189,762.30
01 Sale Price of Property	$180,000.00
02 Sale Price of Any Personal Property Included in Sale	
03 Closing Costs Paid at Closing (J)	$9,682.30
04	
Adjustments	
05	
06	
07	
Adjustments for Items Paid by Seller in Advance	
08 City/Town Taxes to	
09 County Taxes to	
10 Assessments to	
11 HOA Dues 4/15/13 to 4/30/13	$80.00
12	
13	
14	
15	

L. Paid Already by or on Behalf of Borrower at Closing	$175,615.04
01 Deposit	$10,000.00
02 Loan Amount	$162,000.00
03 Existing Loan(s) Assumed or Taken Subject to	
04	
05 Seller Credit	$2,500.00
Other Credits	
06 Rebate from Epsilon Title Co.	$750.00
07	
Adjustments	
08	
09	
10	
11	
Adjustments for Items Unpaid by Seller	
12 City/Town Taxes 1/1/13 to 4/14/13	$365.04
13 County Taxes to	
14 Assessments to	
15	
16	
17	

SELLER'S TRANSACTION

M. Due to Seller at Closing	$180,080.00
01 Sale Price of Property	$180,000.00
02 Sale Price of Any Personal Property Included in Sale	
03	
04	
05	
06	
07	
08	
Adjustments for Items Paid by Seller in Advance	
09 City/Town Taxes to	
10 County Taxes to	
11 Assessments to	
12 HOA Dues 4/15/13 to 4/30/13	$80.00
13	
14	
15	
16	

N. Due from Seller at Closing	$115,665.04
01 Excess Deposit	
02 Closing Costs Paid at Closing (J)	$12,800.00
03 Existing Loan(s) Assumed or Taken Subject to	
04 Payoff of First Mortgage Loan	$100,000.00
05 Payoff of Second Mortgage Loan	
06	
07	
08 Seller Credit	$2,500.00
09	
10	
11	
12	
13	
Adjustments for Items Unpaid by Seller	
14 City/Town Taxes 1/1/13 to 4/14/13	$365.04
15 County Taxes to	
16 Assessments to	
17	
18	
19	

CALCULATION (Borrower)

Total Due from Borrower at Closing (K)	$189,762.30
Total Paid Already by or on Behalf of Borrower at Closing (L)	- $175,615.04
Cash to Close ☒ From ☐ To Borrower	**$14,147.26**

CALCULATION (Seller)

Total Due to Seller at Closing (M)	$180,080.00
Total Due from Seller at Closing (N)	- $115,665.04
Cash ☐ From ☒ To Seller	**$64,414.96**

In the loan closing statement, you can review the summary of all the above, other debits and credits, and how they impact the amount of money you need to bring to closing or the amount of money you will receive at closing. The chart calculating cash to close will provide the final amounts and will also compare if there is any change from the initial loan estimate you received when you began the process.

This example shows a purchase transaction. If it had been a refinance transaction, you would have seen a mortgage payoff before the total cash to close.

Closing

At the closing, all parties sign the documents, and the money is wired as per the contract. If you just purchased a home, you get to possess the home per contract at closing or if you have a separate agreement.

If you refinanced and included cash out, the disbursement will occur three days after closing to give you enough time if you regret and cancel the transaction.

CHAPTER 12: SUMMARY

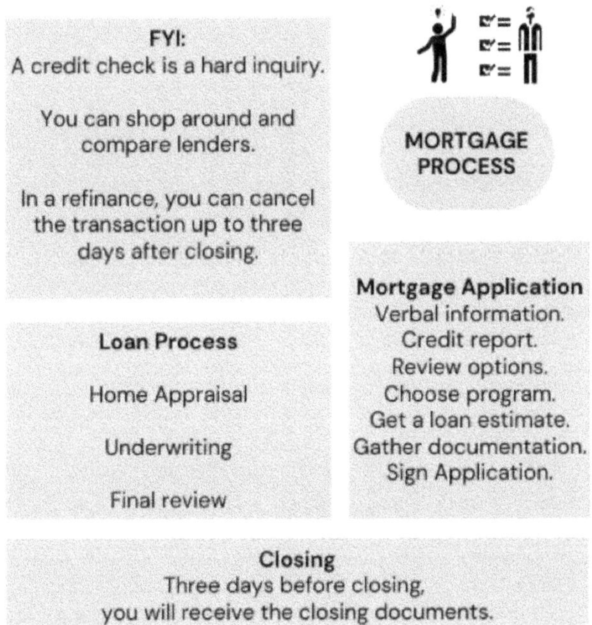

STEP 3 WORKSHEET

- Credit
  - What is your credit score?
  - Is it under 620?
  - Is it above 700?
  - Did you have a bankruptcy? If yes, when?
  - Are there any disputes you can address?
- Income
  - Are you employed, self-employed, or using passive income?
  - Are you employed for more than two years?
  - If you are employed, can you provide the W-2 and the last 60 days of paystubs?
  - If you are self-employed: Are you current with your taxes?
- DTI
  - What is the current DTI?
  - Taking into consideration your personal expenses, what is the DTI you feel comfortable with?
  - Are you looking to consolidate debt?
  - Are you interested in getting cash back from your home equity?
- Assets
  - Do you have savings? How much?
  - If you own a home, what is your LTV?
- VA eligible
  - Are you eligible? Consult your lender.
- USDA eligible
  - Are you eligible? Consult your lender.

STEP 4
THE PURCHASE PROCESS

"The only impossible journey is the one you never begin."
—Tony Robbins

The home purchase process is an emotional yet structured process that can take time or move forward quickly. In the following chapters, we will review the logistics and must-knows when purchasing a property. From the search to your offer and getting under contract, we will cover the entire purchase process up to the closing.

Set your mind up in the present, but do not lose sight of your desired end result. When you find a home, present an offer, and if the seller accepts it, you are under contract, which means just that: you are under contract to purchase a property. The deal can fall apart during the purchase process, so be strategically organized and focused. As we previously reviewed the financial aspects of buying a home, we will focus on the real estate side of the purchase process, omitting the finances, except mentioning when overlapping or needed. Let the search begin.

STEP 4 includes:

Chapter 13:
Home
Search

Chapter 14:
Presenting
an offer

Chapter 15:
Purchase
Process

Home Search

You are ready for this moment, planning what you want and need and putting your finances in order, so what is next? Where is the starting point on this running track? It begins with your team. You might have contacted real estate professionals through different venues, talked with some, and met with others. It is time to decide on the realtor you want to work with.

The realtor can be very resourceful in the search and process, so you must ensure he/she can provide you with the information you need. Knowledge about the area and work experience with the property type you are looking for is a must. In certain areas, there can be meaningful differences in costs, school zones, or other services between properties on the two sides of a street. Some information can impact you in the future, and knowing it now can result in not making an offer on a particular property. I remember touring a house with a client, and everything looked promising. Nearby, some areas were marked as flood zones, but based on the current maps, this property was outside any flood zones. After meeting with a township official, I discovered they were working with a government agency on updating the flood maps and expected to implement the changes in the near future, resulting in the house we were just previewing being in the newly-marked flood zone. If the clients had chosen to proceed, it would have required them to begin paying flood insurance, resulting in a negative factor when deciding to sell the home.

You should work with an honest agent capable of providing objective opinions, as you want a realtor that will prioritize your needs over their financial gain. Excellent communication skills are also essential, as various aspects of these processes are time-sensitive.

When a real estate broker represents you, you will be required to sign an agency agreement with that broker. An exclusive agreement obligates you to use only that brokerage agency, and a nonexclusive agency agreement will allow you to work with several agents. Some agents will not accept working under a nonexclusive agreement. In the agreement itself, be conscious of the period of time you determine this representation will last and under what circumstances you can cancel it.

As for the payment, most realtors' work is based on commissions, and it is common for the seller to pay the buyer's broker commission, but it is not mandatory. In addition, most agency agreements specify under what amount of commission the realtor is not obligated to show you properties. If the commission is under a certain amount, you can be asked to add your commitment to paying additional fees. Those terms of time and fees are negotiable.

Review with your realtor your goals and plans, your wish list, and your must-haves. The realtor will understand better your point of view so the search can be more effective and productive. Knowing your goals will help the realtor determine if one property is more advantageous than another.

Knowing the market

Is your current market a buyer's or seller's market? A buyer's market arises when supply exceeds demand, slowing home sales and reducing home prices. On the contrary, in a seller's market, due to a low inventory of homes, the properties are sold fast, often at the asking price or higher, as there are multiple offers on each property. How does this impact you beyond the home market value?

In a seller's market, everything happens fast. It is common for a house in a seller's market to have multiple showings the first day it hits the market, and if the prospective buyers are interested in the house, they will submit the offer that same day. Listing agents can set up a deadline for when to submit offers, sometimes as soon as two or three days after the house is put on the market. By doing this, the seller's agent creates urgency, and when multiple offers are expected, the seller's agent can request to submit your "best and final" offer. A seller's market will impact the increased sale price, and you can be encouraged to limit or waive repair requests or contract contingencies, all while operating at a fast pace to preview houses, make decisions, and take action. With a buyer's regular weekly work schedule and other commitments, it can be challenging to be available very often, but it might be needed.

A few years ago, I worked as a buyer's agent for a young couple, and it was a very intense seller's market. There was a house they were unsure if they wanted to consider, and on the third day it had been on the market, the clients decided to give it a chance. Their first reaction when entering the home was concern about why the house had been on the market for three days and was not yet under contract. It sounds extreme, but that was the situation back then. They ended up buying a home, and theirs was one of eight offers. It can be very intense, and if the market is such, it is essential to be ready for this pace.

When it is a buyer's market, you have a different range of opportunities. Aside from having a larger inventory, you have an advantage if you make an offer and have no competitors. Your realtor can also find gems in expired listings.

The market's interest rates affect people's willingness and courage to buy houses. During the Covid-19 pandemic, when interest rates were historically low, the real estate market soared, buyers were often in bidding wars, and the properties were usually selling above the asking price. When interest rates increased, the purchase wave cooled, as many buyers preferred waiting until interest rates came down. How is your market? Do you want to buy, and are interest rates high? Are you unsure of the direction to take? You will have an answer if you adhere to the math. On the one hand, when interest rates were low, buyers got a lower interest rate and paid significantly more for their properties. If you find a property you want and interest rates are high, as you do not compete in the same seller's market, can you reduce the purchase price? If you buy the property, can you qualify for the high-interest payments, and is this expense sustainable for you until you refinance your mortgage to lower your interest rates? You can compare how much you would pay additionally with the high-interest rates, to lower interest rates and more expensive purchase prices.

SCENARIO ANALYSIS: PURCHASING A HOME WHEN INTEREST RATES ARE HIGH

Let's compare a current purchase price with a high-interest rate to a future purchase with a lower interest rate.

Purchase price	$300,000
20% down payment	$60,000
Loan amount	$240,000

Monthly payment (P&I) in a 30-year loan:	
7% interest rate	$1,597
6% interest rate	$1,439
5% interest rate	$1,288
4% interest rate	$1,146
3% interest rate	$1,012

Difference in rates (P&I)	Monthly payment:	Total after 1 years	Total after 2 years	Total after 3 years
7% to 3%	$585	$7,020	$14,040	$21,060
7% to 4%	$451	$5,412	$10,824	$16,236
7% to 5%	$309	$3,708	$7,416	$11,124
6% to 5%	$151	$1,812	$3,624	$5,436
6% to 4%	$293	$3,516	$7,032	$10,548
6% to 3%	$427	$5,124	$10,248	$15,372
5% to 4%	$142	$1,704	$3,408	$5,112
5% to 3%	$276	$3,312	$6,624	$9,936

Assume you are buying a property at $300,000 in a high-interest-rate market. If you put a 20% down payment, your monthly P&I payment will vary between $1,012 if you could have a 3% interest rate to $1,597 if you have a 7% interest rate, all in a 30-year loan.

You can decide you are not paying hundreds of dollars more per month, wait until the market stabilizes, and interest rates will decrease. We can assume what interest rates will be in a few years, but for this exercise, let's review the numbers in two and three years. The chart shows you the different options and the total extra payments you make due to the high-interest rates in one, two, and three years. What if you ask the sellers for a discount due to the high-interest rates and buy the property with an upfront discount? At the end of the day, a seller wants to sell, and a buyer wants to buy; some sellers can wait a year or so, and some cannot. If you decide to buy with a high-interest rate, with or without the seller's discount, what is the trend in your area? How much is the property expected to appreciate? You can refinance in a few years or wait a few years to buy with a lower interest rate, but how much will you pay for the property? When interest rates will go down, can you expect multiple offers and above asking price offers? The question is not when will the interest rates go down, rather, in what scenario do you pay less.

How is the inventory where you want to live? What is the migration flow? Are people moving in or out of the area? Your realtor will be able to help you with all this and more. Let the home search begin.

Looking for a property

Your realtor will update you on relevant properties to see. At the same time, you can search online on websites such as zillow.com, and ask your realtor about any properties that interest you. You can attend open houses, and if it is an area you are less familiar with, make sure to drive through at different hours of the day and on weekends.

As you preview properties, if you do not quickly find what you want, do you need to review and prioritize your list of requirements? Do you prefer to reconsider location or other criteria? The home search is dynamic. Aside from having the market much more active in certain months over others, you need to be flexible on the one hand and know your deal breakers on the other hand, as you are the one who will be living on the property in the years to come. Do not let the stress or frustration lead to decisions you will regret.

Be ready and avoid financial surprises

You put effort into ensuring that you are in a good financial situation, as much as possible, to be prepared when you begin the loan application. The effort does not end there. You need to continue until the closing, as often things that appear to have less importance may have a major impact on the process.

A client of mine was on a very tight DTI ratio, and a few days after we began the loan process, the underwriter questioned a new credit card debt. My client opened a store credit card when she went shopping with her daughter, and the store offered a 10% discount on a dress if they paid with a new store credit card. Be aware of the implications of assuming new debt while you are applying for a mortgage.

Prepare your current home

As you are looking for your new home, think about the impact on your current living arrangement and whether there is anything that needs to be done while searching for a new home.

If you are renting, check when your lease expires, and look for solutions according to your specific situation. How much notice should you give in advance? If you are about to renew your lease, check if it can be month-to-month. This means that you need to provide a month's notice as the lease is renewed monthly.

If you own a home, do you plan on renting it after moving out or selling it, and what is your preference or need regarding the period of time while you hold the two properties and do not sell or rent your current home?

Can you begin making the transition easier?

Some tasks, such as decluttering, can be very time-consuming and, on the other hand, very beneficial at this stage. It does not matter if you screen your belongings and donate some or pack items that are not needed for immediate use. I prefer to use same-size boxes (with some exceptions for larger items) to appear organized, save space while packing, and store them in the basement or garage.

Is there anything you can do now that will present your home in the best possible light when it is the right time? For example, if you plan to have professional painters work in your house after you move out, you need to wait. If you want to do it yourself, remove personal pictures and paint areas by sections.

Are there any known repairs needed? There is an option to sell the house, and note that certain items are as-is, meaning they might not work, and you do not intend to repair them. If an item needs repair, it is better to schedule that in advance to be more flexible with the professional's availability and to have the time to compare different bids.

Eventually, you will find the home you want. Are you ready to make an offer?

CHAPTER 13: SUMMARY

Prepare
Avoid financial surprises.
Time availability.
Prepare your current home.

Know Your Market

Wish List
Revise your needs and wants. Prioritize.

CHAPTER 14

Presenting an Offer

When you are ready to make an offer, plan your strategy with your realtor, as there are a few things to elaborate on before writing down the offer.

What do you know about the seller? Understanding the seller's preferences will help you present a stronger offer. For example, if the seller would prefer to move out in three months, it will not be in your favor to offer a fast closing unless you are interested in closing and letting the seller rent back the home from you for a few months. Suppose a seller is in a rush, unavailable, or not interested in doing any repairs. In that case, an as-is contract will allow you to stand out if a competitor requires inspections and repairs even though the property is not for sale strictly in as-is condition. Some sellers would like the highest sale price, and others are emotionally attached to the house, and a cover letter from the buyer can go a long way.

Do you have competition? Did the seller receive other offers? The listing agent can update your realtor if he/she is expecting, waiting to review, or on a specific timeline related to other offers.

For the current time and place, what are your boundaries, what is a must, and what is a deal breaker specifically to this property? It might be that you began your active search a week ago, and you are ready to make an offer. Probably, your timeline aligns with what you spoke with your realtor about the previous week. If time has passed by since the initial search, review your timeline, and determine if there are any features in the property that you need to be aware of immediately, whether to ask for clarification from the listing agent before presenting an offer or if there is something that requires you to take action immediately after offer acceptance. Is this property aligned with the initial budget planned? If it is needed to increase the price offer, are you open to this, or did you decide to begin with the best and final offer from your end?

From an offer to under contract

When writing the offer, different terms need to be decided, in addition to the price.

- Dates: When do you expect to close?

- Price: What is the purchase price, how much are you offering to pay **earnest money** (EM), when will you deliver the EM, and to whom?

- As-Is Condition: This is used when a house is dated or when a seller is unwilling or prefers not to make any repairs before closing. The market value of a house sold in as-is condition is less than a house in mint condition, subject to inspection. There are cases where the house is not in a bad condition, but the sellers prefer an as-is offer because they are looking to close faster. If you want to go this path, you can still perform inspections, and it can be marked in the as-is contract that buyers will do inspections for their knowledge only to ensure you are allowed to perform the inspections.

- **Inspection Rider**: When the sale is subject to inspection, it means that after you receive the inspection report, you will review what needs to be repaired, and you will prioritize any repair requests from the seller. Usually, the buyer has ten days to complete the inspections and respond to the seller with any requests. You should plan to have the inspection report as soon as possible to have enough time to review the report, prioritize the items marked, and ask for professional repair estimates if necessary. When a buyer responds to the seller, if there are items that need to be addressed, the buyer can ask for them to be repaired, or get a credit for the cost of the repairs. For example, if the inspector has marked some electrical issues, the buyer can ask a licensed electrician for an estimate of the cost of the repair. The buyer can ask the seller to repair the electrical items or get a credit (discount) for the amount of the repair, as specified in the estimate attached. The seller, in return, needs to respond if he/she accepts the requests, counteroffers what he/she is willing to do, or rejects the requests.

What should a buyer ask for? It all depends on the market. Often, sellers will address any structural or hazard issue; if they do not address it, they are obligated to disclose it to any future buyer. Other plumbing, electrical, operational, or cosmetic issues can be open to negotiations.

- **Appraisal Rider**: This gives the homebuyer the option to back out of the purchase contract if the property fails to appraise to a minimum of the sale's price. In this case, the buyer can either renegotiate the sale price with the seller or back out of the contract. It is important to understand this, as in a seller's market, when there are multiple offers expected, you might want to offer above the asking price, but be sure to understand what it means if your offer is accepted. If the home is appraised at a lower amount than the offer, and you maxed out the loan amount option, you might need to bring more money to the closing table.

♦ Specifics about fixtures and other items: The seller can mark an item as excluded (for example, a chandelier), and you can ask a specific item to be included (for example, a pool table).

A fixture is an object permanently attached to the property and will remain in the house, such as a ceiling fan or a window treatment. Items not attached to the property are not required to remain unless specified in writing in the contract. Do not assume an item is included unless it is cleared and in writing.

I want to share with you a personal experience. A few years ago, we bought a house with a playset in the yard. It was attached to the ground, so it was considered a fixture. About three months after the sale, I saw a man I did not know, in my yard, on top of the playset. He had just finished disassembling the roof of the slide, and he was ready to continue disassembling the playset. I was distraught; I stepped outside, and he told me that the previous owner had sent him to take the playset. I called the seller, and she confirmed that she sent the man to take the playset; she assumed that I would not want it because I did not have young children, and so she saw no need to specify it in the contract. Please, do not assume. As for the playset, it remained on my property.

♦ Seller's Response Time: This indicates the deadline the seller has to respond to the offer, and if there is no response by the deadline, the offer is no longer valid.

With the offer, your realtor will guide you about the documentation needed, such as a preapproval letter and other documentation usually attached to the offer.

The sellers can respond to your offer with rejection, acceptance, or counteroffer.

In a counteroffer, the seller can address any terms, such as the price, the closing date, and you can accept, reject, or counteroffer back in response to the seller.

After the terms are agreed upon between the seller and the buyer, and the sale contract is signed by all parties, you are officially under contract and the clock begins ticking toward your closing.

Let's continue with the purchase process from the moment you are under contract.

CHAPTER 14: SUMMARY

Presenting An Offer
What does the seller want?
How is your market
Timeline, contingencies,
and offer's strength.

From An Offer To Under contract

CHAPTER 15

Purchase Process

When an offer is accepted, is the sale transaction guaranteed? No. Theoretically, if everything goes as planned, you will be good to close. The reality is that there are a few aspects you do not control. The mortgage needs to be approved, and you will review the inspection report to decide if any items need to be negotiated with the seller. The appraisal report will be delivered with a specific value, and if the property does not appraise at the expected value, you will review your options according to the terms set up in the sale contract. The **title** company will do the title search and provide you with a copy of the **title insurance**. You will look for a home insurance company and confirm that you can insure the home.

Contract's Timeline

You need to be on top of the timeline of the items required, as the agreement defines the time to address each aspect of the contract. If there are any changes, they must be in writing and signed by all parties involved. Once an agreement is accepted, your realtor will guide you on what actions need to be taken, such as working with a title company to begin the title search, title insurance, etc.

I would like to focus on three things you need to do immediately:

♦ Check the due date to deposit the earnest money.

The earnest money, also called a good faith deposit, is an up-front deposit made by the buyer, and the sale contract specifies where the deposit is held. It can be the seller's broker escrow account or a third party, such as a title company's escrow account. The contract will specify how many business days you have to deposit the earnest money. Usually, the buyer is required to deposit 1%-3% of the purchase price in an escrow account. Sometimes it is divided into two deposits: the first deposit is several days after the contract is accepted (usually three to five days), and the other portion is a certain number of days after the inspection stage is concluded (after the negotiations post-inspection report, if the property is not sold as-is). You do have a few days for the initial deposit, but you need to be aware of this to ensure that you have the money available and to provide the check to your realtor so that he/she can deliver it to the entity that will deposit the check into the escrow account.

Timing is critical. You must be aware of the deadlines and not be in a breach of contract because you planned to do something over the weekend and missed the due date.

- ♦ If you plan on doing a home inspection, contact a home inspector and schedule the inspection.

Often, inspectors are not immediately available, and you usually have ten days to provide the addendum with any repair requests based on the inspection report. This means that you need time to coordinate with the inspector and time for the inspector to submit the inspection report. Based on the inspection report, you review with your realtor if there is any aspect that you want to address with the seller.

In a property sale contract, you have a section that specifies the inspection period. If you choose the option of a special sale contract, where the property is sold as-is, you can still request on the contract that the buyer will do inspections "for the buyer's knowledge only." This means that you waive the inspection **contingency** but do not waive the right to do an inspection.

When you waive the inspection contingency, you are not expected to ask the seller to address any cosmetic or other minor repairs. However, you still keep the right to return to the seller if there are any significant hazard findings, such as mold, radon gas, asbestos, structural problems, etc.

- ♦ As soon as an offer is accepted, you should choose your lender and initiate the loan process. Contact your lender, review the loan terms, decide if you are shopping around to compare the terms of the loan, and after deciding with which lender you want to work, lock in the interest rate and begin the mortgage application process as soon as possible.

In a standard sale contract, you need to choose between two options:

Not contingent upon financing
Contingent upon financing

A not contingent upon financing option means that the sale is not contingent upon a loan's approval. This can be when a buyer offers a cash sale, or even if the buyer plans to finance the deal with a lender's mortgage, the buyer can't cancel the sale because a lender rejected his loan application.

A contingent upon financing option means that the buyer has a set number of days to secure the loan, usually 30 days unless stated differently on the sale contract, and if the buyer delivers the written notice from the lender stating that the loan request is denied in the time frame stated in the agreement, the buyer is protected by the contingency clause. This is why the buyer needs to rush the process as much as possible, especially since certain aspects are beyond his/ her control, as the home appraisal.

Because we do not know how much a day or two can affect the timeline, always proceed with urgency, so there is more time, if needed, to address unexpected occurrences.

Inspections and due diligence

Your realtor can help you coordinate the required inspections. The inspections will help you determine any work needed, regardless of whether or not you ask the seller to address it.

If you plan to buy a dated home and do an extensive renovation, you do not need to pay for a regular inspection. It is not useful to have an inspector mark that there is no silicone caulking around the toilet if you intend to do a bathroom demolition. It can be beneficial to have the plumbing checked, review if any basement cracks need to be examined further, check the roof and mechanics, or perform other inspections that can clarify the actual condition of the home.

In addition, are any pending open permits? In some cases, the township will have this information. In others, the county will provide it.

The seller will provide you with a seller's disclosure, where the sellers will mark everything they know about the physical condition of the house, and in the section where the seller is asked if there were renovations done in the home, he/she will be asked if a permit was issued or not. The seller should provide the most accurate information to the best of his/her knowledge. Sometimes, the seller is unaware of whether a previous home addition had a permit. Why is this important? It will be more convenient for you not to have surprises down the road.

It has happened to me that I have found open permits. Once, a previous seller submitted a permit, the inspection failed, and the buyer continued and finished the work, in this case, a retaining wall, without the required inspections to approve and close the open permit. In other cases, there were home additions with no records of permits in the past. In that case, I confirmed with the authorities that it was grandfathered, which means that the addition does not have to comply with existing zoning or building codes because it was legally built before those requirements were enforced. What it means for a buyer is that he will not have legal challenges while owning the home and will not have a problem selling the home in the future.

Appraisal

The appraisal is ordered by the lender, and it must be conducted by a third party for legal purposes. When the appraiser submits his report to the lender, the lender will compare the appraised value to the sale price, or the estimated home value, if you are refinancing. Address any changes, if required, if the appraised value is higher or lower than what you anticipated.

Title

A property **title** reflects all the legal rights related to the ownership and use of the property. The title company conducts a title search, assuring the rights of the seller on the property, and they check the chain of title from the moment the property was built up to the last owner, the current seller, to assure that you will receive a title with no disputes and no other claims for the title. **Title insurance** protects the property owners and the lender against any property loss or damage due to liens, encumbrances, or defects in the property's title.

Homeowners Insurance

Begin shopping around. You will be surprised by how different the quotes can be. If you decide to escrow the payment for the home insurance, remember that escrow is only the payment method. You have the legal right to choose any insurance company you want, and as the years pass by, continue to be aware of the cost as the market shifts. A good solution one year may not necessarily be a good option a few years down the road. A few months ago, my husband contacted our home insurance company and asked them why our renewal increased by more than 100%, and the sales representative told my husband that the company had a very bad year, so they needed to make it up. I thought my husband was joking that this was the insurance company's response. He was not. Of course, we changed to a different home insurance company, and our new premium decreased from the previous year's payment. Always shop around and compare costs and coverage.

Preparing for closing

After all the requirements are fulfilled, all the reviews, inspections, and underwriting are done; when you are told that you are ready to close, it means that all the approvals were concluded and you are prepared to set up the closing date and the location.

What needs to be done or reviewed just days before the closing, and what must you be aware of to get to that desired point?

Closing Disclosure

A closing disclosure is prepared by a settlement agent and lists all commissions and costs in addition to the net total to be paid to the seller.

Closing statements will include the parties involved, property details and financial information, the purchase price of the home, deposits paid by the buyer, seller's credits, prorated amounts, and loan costs. The final closing disclosure should be delivered at least three days before closing.

A final walkthrough

Before closing, you should do a walkthrough of the property. During the walk, you should look around and confirm that everything looks as expected. For example, all fixtures, such as kitchen appliances, light fixtures, and window treatments, should still be present in the house. Regardless of the visual inspection, before the walkthrough, the seller must provide receipts for all of the required repairs he/she committed to do. If something is different than expected, this is the time to clarify this. The closing can be postponed until the issue is addressed, or an amount of money required for a specific repair can be held in escrow, and you can choose to continue with the closing.

Sometimes, there are external factors beyond our control. For example, if the weather is under a specific temperature, the air conditioning unit might not be able to be inspected, and exterior painting cannot be performed. The goal is to address all possible situations and solutions before you get to the closing table.

Closing

At the closing, you execute the real estate transaction. On the closing day, ownership is transferred from the seller to the buyer.

The seller and the buyer do not have to meet in a sale transaction. As the final transaction details are sent to the seller and buyer three days before closing, on the day of closing, the seller typically signs the closing documents first, and afterwards, the buyer signs all the documents and transfers the money.

CHAPTER 15: SUMMARY

Inspections   Appraisal
Lender's approval   Title
Homeowners' Insurance
A final walkthrough
Closing disclosure   Closing

STEP 4 WORKSHEET

Searching for a home:
- ♦ What is your market? A seller's or a buyer's market?
- ♦ Do you have the type of homes you want in your desired area?

What is the urgency of the purchase:
- ♦ You need to buy by a certain date, even overpriced?
- ♦ Do you have an absolute maximum price, regardless of the home fixtures?

Home offer:
- ♦ What are your must haves?
- ♦ Price
- ♦ Dates
- ♦ Contingencies
- ♦ Other Special requests

In the purchase process, what are your must haves?
- ♦ Appraisal value
- ♦ Repairs following inspections
- ♦ Timeline
- ♦ Other

STEP 5
YOUR DIRECTION

"Setting goals is the first step in turning the invisible into the visible." —Tony Robbins.

Congratulations! You have gotten to this point. You read and worked all the way to reach this final step. In the introduction, I presented the dilemma of whether or not you were getting correct answers to the wrong questions. The very common approach of asking *how much can I qualify for* at the beginning of a home loan process should be replaced with the questions such as: *what are my goals, how much do I want to spend, how much should I invest, and in what venues?* Many more questions will come along the way, but the most important lesson is finding the time to pause, dream, think, plan, and define what you really want. Your property should, in addition to being your home, give you pride, comfort, and a tool you can leverage to achieve your financial goals.

As you worked through the worksheets of the first four steps, you had to deal with questions you did not necessarily have the answers to, and others added work to your ever-expanding to-do list. After defining your goals and paths, you will periodically update and adjust your course. It is an active, lifelong process.

When defining what you want, express your desires in the most simple, specific, and measurable way. Generalities will end up just being that; generally vague. The same applies to quantifying what you want and when you want it. Hard work and delayed gratification can be encouraged by achieving milestones in your timeline, affirming that you are moving forward toward achieving your goals. When planning, do not fall into the analysis-paralysis mode, as you can find yourself unable to decide due to overthinking and endlessly pouring over the upsides and downsides of each option, making you unable to pick any course of action.

You may find that many articles, lecturers, and personal opinions contradict each other at any time. Is it the right time to buy, or should you wait? Some will advise you to wait until the market shifts, others will advise you not to wait as you will miss an opportunity, and many more scenarios. My suggestion is to stick to the numbers. Working on the numbers will give you a better idea of your options while clearing your decisions from the emotional impact of either excitement or fear. The best solutions are not exclusively the ones with the highest profitability. If a solution sounds theoretically good, but it will add enormous financial constraints on you, is it worth it? Measure your risks.

Make your plan realistic. In this final step, you will write down and draft your plan!

MY WEALTH

Can you summarize what wealth means to you in one or two sentences?

Wealth

MY GOALS

To narrow your plan down, define more specific measurable goals. Are you looking to achieve a specific equity amount? If yes, how much? Are you looking to live with no mortgage or rent expenses? Are you looking for passive income? How much? Do you want to have enough money to purchase something?

Goals

MY PROPERTY

Do you have a dream property? An end-result purchase?

Based on all that you know, what will be your living arrangements for the next three to five years? Will you rent or buy? Single-family, condo, or multi-family? Stay in your current residence and refinance if needed?

Property

MY PATH

What is the path you want to take? Use your home more passively or actively?

Based on your desired destination, what journey do you want to take? Home hacking? Rental income or home appreciation and profit when selling? How would you quantify each goal?

My path

MILESTONES and TIMELINE

Decide what factors guide your decisions.

Is it financial, family, your own's milestones, or something else? What is the timeline to achieve your goals, and what are the milestones to review?

Milestones and timeline

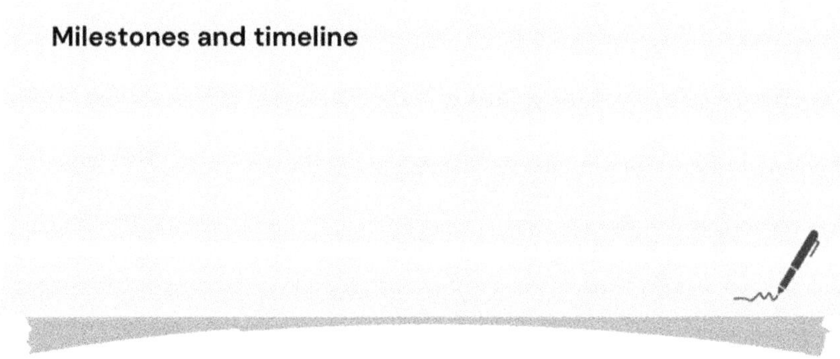

GETTING TO MY STARTING POINT

Map out your current situation. Use the summaries from the previous chapters.

If you are currently renting:

- When does the lease end?
- How much is the monthly expense?
- What next step will benefit you the most?

If you own a home:

- Did the value of your home increase since you purchased it or your last refinance?
- How long do you plan to stay in the home? Does your exit strategy need to be re-evaluated?
- Is your mortgage fulfilling your current goals?

Prioritize three things you think can benefit you.

What do you feel holds you back?

Starting point

Remember, "Life does not get better by chance;
it gets better by change"—Jim Rohn

Focus on the destination. Enjoy your journey.
Leverage your home. Strategize your money.
Achieve all your American Dreams.

www.AskOrli.com

Glossary

Adjustable Rate Mortgage (ARM): In a mortgage with an ARM interest rate, the rate changes during the life of a loan.

After Repair Value (ARV): The estimated value of a property after completing planned renovations.

Amortization: A plan of paying off debt in equal installments. A fully amortized loan means your loan will be fully paid off by the end of the term.

Amortization Schedule: A chart showing the breakdown of your monthly payment, how much goes to pay principal, and how much goes to pay interest.

Amortized Loan: When a loan is paid down over the life of the loan.

Appraisal (Home): An expert estimate of the home's value.

Appraisal Rider: In a home purchase transaction, if your home does not appraise for the amount you have agreed upon, you can walk away from the deal, keeping your deposit.

Appreciation: In real estate, it is the increased value of a property over a period of time.

Balloon mortgage: When the mortgage is not fully amortized over the term of the loan, and there is a balance due when the final repayment of the loan is due.

Capital gain (Home): Profits from selling capital assets, in this case, a home.

Cash-Out Refinance: Occurs when a new loan is taken on a property already owned. The new loan amount will cover the payoff of the existing loan, any loan expenses, and the balance will be paid in cash to the owner.

Closing: This is the final step in executing a real estate transaction; purchasing or refinancing a property. When purchasing a property, on the closing day, property ownership is transferred from the seller to the buyer.

Closing costs: Fees and expenses you pay when you buy a property or secure a loan.

Closing statement / Closing disclosure: Is a document that records the details of a financial transaction.

Closing table: In some areas of the country, real estate settlement is completed at what is known as a "closing table." Closing involves several people. Typically, the buyer, the seller, and the lender attend the closing. A real estate attorney, settlement agent, or title agent may conduct the closing.

Comparative Market Analysis (CMA): Realtors use the comparison method of similar properties in the area to estimate a property's value.

Condo / Condominium: A building containing a number of individually owned apartments.

Contingency: A contract provision that requires a specific event or action to take place for the contract to be considered valid.

Conventional loan: A loan that is not a government backed or secured loan.

Co-sign: A co-signer takes full responsibility for paying back a loan, along with the primary borrower. The co-signer is obligated to pay any missed payments and even the loan balance if the borrower doesn't pay.

Credit bureaus: Companies that collect information about individuals' credit history. Equifax, Experian, and Transunion are the three major credit bureaus in the U.S.

Credit cards' credit limit: The maximum amount the financial institution or lender extends to the debtor.

Credit card minimum monthly payment: The least amount the debtor needs to pay on a set due date.

Credit report: A document that records the borrower's credit history. It is provided by the credit bureaus.

Credit score: A prediction of your credit behavior, such as how likely you are to pay a loan back on time, based on information from your credit reports.

Debt-to-income (DTI): The percentage of the consumer's monthly gross income allocated to pay debts.

Depreciation: The reduction in an asset's value over time due to wear and tear.

Discount points: Are fees a homebuyer pays directly to the lender in exchange for a reduced interest rate.

Down payment: The cash the buyer pays upfront in a real estate transaction. Down payments are typically a percentage of the purchase price.

Earnet Money (EM): The sum of money you deposit in escrow, usually a few days after signing the purchase agreement or the sales contract.

Escrow: In a mortgage, your lender will set up a mortgage escrow account where part of your monthly payment is deposited to cover some of the costs associated with home ownership, such as real estate taxes, home insurance premiums, and private mortgage insurance costs.

Equity: The difference between the property value and the debts on the property.

FHA: Mortgage insured by the US Federal Housing Administration.

Fixed interest rate loan: A loan where the interest rate doesn't fluctuate.

Government-backed loans: A loan subsidized by the government, which protects lenders against defaults on payments, thus making it much easier for lenders to offer potential borrowers lower interest rates.

Government-insured loans: A loan insured by the government to guarantee repayment to the bank should you default on your mortgage payment.

Home inspection: A process that observes and reports on the condition of a real estate property, usually when it is on the market to be sold. It is common for the buyer to order the inspection at their own expense.

Homeowner's association (HOA): An organization in a subdivision, planned community, or condominium building that makes and enforces rules for the properties and residents.

Homeowners insurance: A form of property insurance that covers losses and damages to an individual's house and assets in the home. The policy usually covers interior damage, exterior damage, loss or damage of personal assets, and injury that arises while on the property.

Homestead: The house and adjoining land where the owner primarily resides. Legally, what constitutes a homestead varies from state to state. Properties that qualify as homesteads may also benefit from homestead exemptions, which can offer homeowners certain financial and legal protections.

Home warranty: A contract that agrees to provide a homeowner with discounted repair and replacement services.

House/Home hacking: Finding ways to generate income from your home, such as buying a multifamily property, living in one unit, and renting the others.

Inspection Rider: Is a clause in a purchase contract that makes the success of the sale contingent upon the home inspection results. It protects the buyer if, as deriving from the home inspection, they do not want to go forward with the sale.

Interest: The price you pay to borrow money. It is an annual percentage of the loan's amount.

Jumbo loan: A home loan for an amount that exceeds the "conforming loan limit" set on mortgages eligible for purchase by Fannie Mae and Freddie Mac.

Loan estimate: Three-page form you receive within three days after a lender pulls your credit as part of inquiring about a mortgage. It details the suggested loan's terms.

Loan to value (LTV): The ratio of the mortgage as a percentage of the total appraised value of a real estate.

Market value: How much a home will sell for, under normal conditions, in the current market.

Minimum monthly payment: The lowest monthly amount required to pay back a loan, by a certain due date.

Mortgage: An agreement between you and a lender that allows you to borrow money to purchase or refinance a home.

Mortgage insurance premium (MIP): An upfront and monthly insurance premium is required with an FHA loan.

Mortgage insurance: Lowers the risk to the lender of making a loan to you, so you can qualify for a loan that you might not otherwise be able to get. Typically, in a conventional loan, borrowers making a down payment of less than 20% of the home's purchase price will need to pay mortgage insurance.

Mortgage refinance: Replacing the mortgage you have with a new mortgage that has more favorable terms.

Multi-family: Any residential property containing more than one housing unit. A duplex or apartment complex is an example of a multi-family home.

Owner-occupied property: A home in which the person who holds the title (or owns the property) also uses it as their primary residence.

Primary residence: Your home, also known as a principal residence. Whether it's a house, condo, or townhome, if you take up occupancy for most of the year and can prove it, it's your primary residence.

Principal: The balance of the amount you borrowed and have to pay back.

Private Mortgage Insurance (PMI): Type of mortgage insurance you might be required to pay, in a conventional loan.

Refinance: Replacing your mortgage with a new one with more favorable terms.

Recast: Mortgage recast is when you make additional payments towards your principal, and the lender will reamortize your mortgage with the new balance.

Single-family: A free-standing residential property. Single-family homes are designed to be used as single-dwelling units with no shared walls and land.

Tax deductible: For tax purposes, a deductible is an expense that an individual taxpayer or a business can subtract from adjusted gross income while completing a tax form. The deductible expense reduces taxable income and, therefore, the income taxes owed.

Tax exclusion: Income that is approved to be excluded from the amount of money you file as your gross income, ultimately reducing the total amount of taxes you owe for the year.

Tax exemptions: The right to exclude all or some income from taxation by federal or state governments.

Terms of a loan: Terms and conditions involved when borrowing money. A loan term is the amount of time you have to repay your loan.

Title: An intangible construct representing a bundle of rights in a piece of property, and a party may own legal or equitable interest.

Title insurance: Protects real estate owners and lenders against property loss or damage due to liens, encumbrances, or defects in the property's title.

USDA: A mortgage loan offered to rural property owners, by the Unites States Department of Agriculture.

Veteran Administration (VA) loan: A mortgage loan guaranteed by the US Department of Veteran Affairs.

Acknowledgments

RONEN, MY HUSBAND, THANK YOU FOR
BELIEVING IN ME AND SUPPORTING MY PATHS
DESPITE ALL THE SURROUNDING NOISES.

My boys, thank you for your support. Shay, I appreciate your help and love of the English language. You definitely chose the path less traveled. Yaniv, my partner in crime, I enjoy speaking with you for hours about real estate, annoying and boring everyone around us. Thank you for your professional input and support. Amir, thanks for challenging me to write another book, as you prefer not to read about surrealism art, in Spanish.

Dean Graziosi and Tony Robbins, on your inspiration and lighting the spark.

Steve Harrison and the team, and special thanks to Debby Englander, Cristina Smith, Christy Day, Kim Cruse, Valerie Costa, Steve Scholl, and Maggie McLaughlin. Thank you for your incredible support on this fascinating path.

My friends, whose valuable input helped shape this book, and special thanks to Brooke and Garry Wolfe, Galit Lev-Harir, Steve Safran, and Arza Raviv.